this journal belongs to

Table of Contents

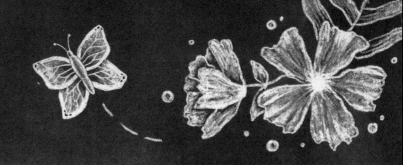

Introduction

Hey there, beautiful girl!

I am beyond grateful and excited that you're here! You are living through a monumental season of life and God has a plan and a purpose for placing you on this planet at this exact time in history. You are not here by accident, nor are the people around you. No matter what season you face, either now or in the future, there is always hope because you have a God that loves you and cares for you!

The Bible is a big book. In my teen years, I remember feeling a bit over-whelmed by the size of it. I often used the "close your eyes, pray, and flip to a random page" strategy, hoping that I would open to an impactful verse. While this method got me reading my Bible, it didn't allow for substantial growth in my faith. I'd also highlight certain verses shared at my church and youth group but still found it challenging to dive into the Bible on my own. I was always encouraged to pray and talk to God, which felt easier, but even my prayer life felt a bit jumbled at times.

I learned about the concordance section of my Bible in my teens and it was a significant part of my spiritual growth. Not all Bibles have a concordance, but for the ones that do, it's typically in the back. You can use it as a reference for looking up specific words and verses. Words are listed alphabetically, and under each word is a list of verses containing that particular word and where you can find them in the Bible. This is especially helpful for journaling and topic study. The internet can also be used as a resource for looking up specific words and verses.

Your teen years are a very special time in your life. You are a rising generation of influence, and you have an opportunity to make an impact for God's Kingdom right where He's placed you, even at your young age. Scripture is full of stories of how God worked through young people, regardless of their age and experience, and He can absolutely use you, too. My hope and my prayer is that you use this journal to share your thoughts, prayers, and anything that's on your heart with God, and that as you do, your faith will be strengthened. He's always listening!

Your journal is set up so that you are introduced to new scriptures, reflections, and journaling spaces each week. You'll be able to record your prayers to God throughout the year, and keep track of when and how He answers them. After the year is over, you'll be able to look back and see the incredible ways God has moved *with you* over the year.

No matter what your background is, the season of life you're in, or the ups and downs you've experienced, there's a place for you here. God loves you so much and desires a loving relationship with you. He is always at work and promises to work all things out for the good of those who love Him (Romans 8:28). That includes you!

Welcome to this journey! And thank you for allowing me to be a small part of your walk with our almighty God and Savior. I pray you grow closer to God throughout your journaling experience and that He blesses you beyond measure!

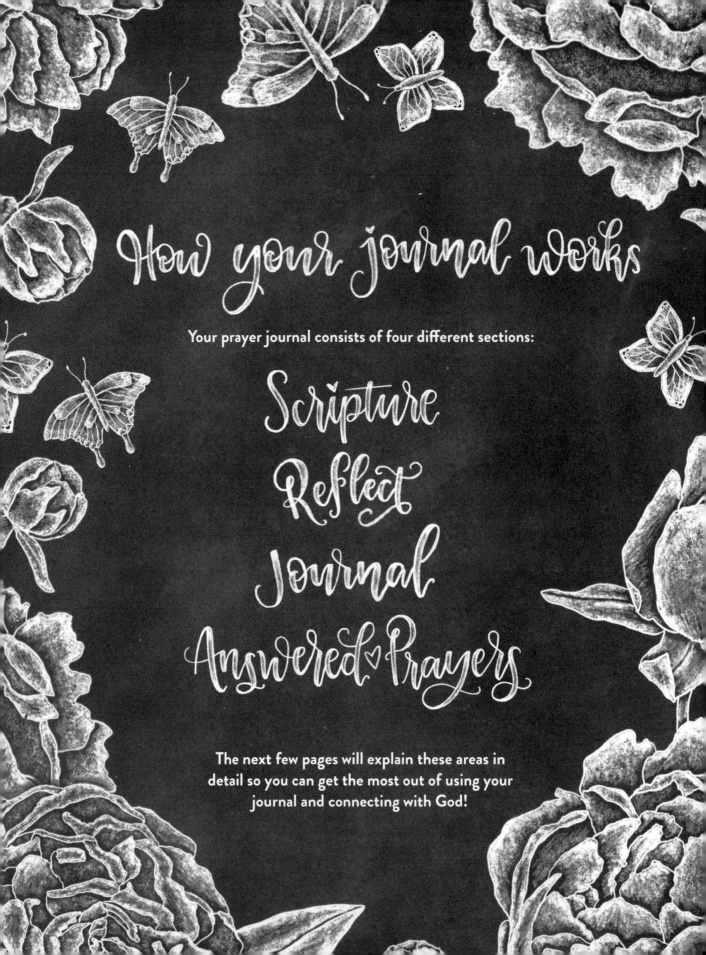

How your journal works

Your prayer journal consists of four different sections:

Scripture

Reflect

Journal

Answered ♡ Prayers

The next few pages will explain these areas in detail so you can get the most out of using your journal and connecting with God!

Scripture

Each week, you will have a new verse to reflect and meditate on throughout your week. Some verses are longer than others, but the more you read and revisit each verse, the more familiar you will become with it! Giving you a week per verse will allow you more time to memorize and ingrain the verse into your heart and mind!

JOSHUA 1:9

Have I not commanded you? Be *strong and courageous*. Do not be afraid; do not be discouraged, for the Lord your *God will be with you* wherever you go.

LOVE

HOPE

faith

Reflect

FEAR

The unknown can be scary. From those jitters you get on the first day of school, to the nerves you get before a big performance or game, it's perfectly natural to feel uncertain and insecure when you're about to embark on something new. But God knew you would experience fear in the face of new things. He calls you to be strong and courageous because He will *never* leave you.

In Scripture, Joshua had big shoes to fill when God called him to succeed Moses in leading the Israelites to the Promised Land. Joshua had witnessed the hardships, trials, and rebellion, as well as the blessings the Israelites encountered as Moses led God's people out of Egypt and wandered in the desert for 40 years looking for the Promised Land. Even though Joshua had been trained by Moses and loved and trusted God, the task was a big one. But God promised to be with Joshua wherever he went, in whatever he did. And He promises the same for you. No matter what path the Lord takes you on in your life, He is always there walking the journey with you. His blessings and reassurances are all around—on beautiful walks in nature, in the promises you hear in worship music and in Scripture, within the friends and loved ones He's surrounded you with, and more. God loves you and He will never leave you, nor forsake you!

Do new things scare you? What new things is God calling you to right now? Share about a time you felt God's presence as you courageously embarked on something new.

Reflect

Each week also includes a "Reflect" page, with thoughts and questions prompted by the weekly Scripture and space for you to record your thoughts and responses. You may use this as an ongoing weekly reflection or fill the space in a single day! Fill this space as your schedule allows and as you feel comfortable doing so!

Journal

Record the date or week it is.

Use this space to continue journaling your thoughts from the reflection on the previous page.

What are you thankful for this week? Let God know how grateful you are for His blessings in your life.

Reflection continued . . .

Date

LORD, thank you

You did not choose me, but I chose you and appointed you so that you might go and bear fruit—fruit that will last—and so that whatever you ask in my name the Father will give you.

JOHN 15:16

Things on my heart

Highlights

Prayer requests

Each week includes a special verse that is specifically about prayer with the aim to encourage you on your prayer journey with the Lord.

What is on your heart this week? What things are tugging on your heart and occupying your mind?

Record your prayers. This can be done in one sitting or at various times throughout your week. Don't forget to record new prayers in the back of the book in the "Answered Prayers" section!

Life is fast-paced and non-stop at times. Take time to write down and record the special, precious things that happen during your day-to-day each week.

Answered Prayers

In the back of the book, there is an area to record your prayers. This will allow you to keep track of how God answers your prayers this year!

Every time you write a new prayer request in your weekly journaling "Prayer requests" section, be sure to flip to the back of the book to record it.

Each time you record a new prayer request, be sure to write down the date at the same time. This way, you can keep track of when you first started praying for a specific prayer request.

Once a prayer has been answered, record the date! At the end of the year, you'll be able to look back at all the prayer requests God answered!

Table of Contents

Your table of contents serves as a guide for what's in your prayer journal. There is no wrong way of navigating through it. Some will prefer to start at the beginning, while others will prefer to skip around each week. The box next to each week serves as a way to keep track of which verses and devotions you've completed. You can add a check in the box after finishing each week (if you go in order) or a number if you prefer to skip around and keep track of which devotions you've done. (Example: for week 1, place a 1 in the box, rather than a checkmark.)

Glossary

The Bible is full of words and terms that aren't always easy to understand. Use this page as a resource when you get stuck on a particular word you might not know. Words are listed alphabetically.

ADVERSITY: going through difficult or hard times

APOSTLE: a messenger with a mission; in Scripture, the apostles were messengers of God who went out to spread the gospel of Jesus Christ

ATONEMENT: the payment for wrongdoing in order to make amends and reconcile; in Scripture, Jesus paid the price for our sins through His death and resurrection so that we could be reconciled to God

DISCIPLE: a person who learns from another; in Scripture, the twelve disciples were taught by Jesus

GRACE: unmerited favor; in Scripture, God sent Jesus to die on the cross for the sins of humanity, not because we earned it, but because He loves us

LINEAGE: the line of descendants coming from an ancestor or past relative

MERCY: the result of compassion or forgiveness toward someone who could otherwise be punished or harmed; God demonstrated his mercy for us by sending Jesus to die on the cross for our sins so that through our faith and acceptance of Him, we could be reconciled to God

NEW TESTAMENT: the second part of the Christian Bible (written in Greek) that discusses the life of Jesus and Christianity in the early church; made up of 27 books

OLD TESTAMENT: the first part of the Christian Bible (written primarily in Hebrew) ; made up of 39 books

PERSEVERE: to keep going despite hardship or difficulty

PROPHET: a person that is inspired by God and speaks on behalf of Him

PROVISION: the act of providing or supplying something

SALVATION: in Christianity, salvation comes from faith, repentance, and acceptance of Jesus Christ as one's Savior; it is the state of being saved or protected from sin's consequences

SOVEREIGNTY: supreme authority and power; God is sovereign over His creation

THE GOSPELS: the New Testament books of Matthew, Mark, Luke, and John that recount the life of Jesus Christ and His ministry on Earth

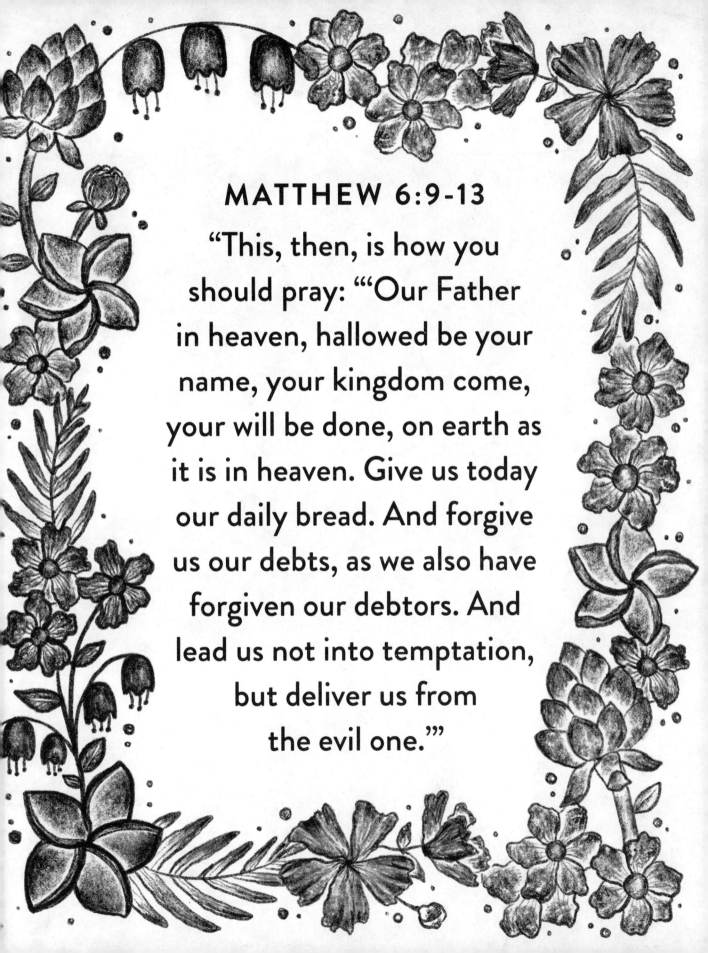

MATTHEW 6:9-13

"This, then, is how you should pray: "'Our Father in heaven, hallowed be your name, your kingdom come, your will be done, on earth as it is in heaven. Give us today our daily bread. And forgive us our debts, as we also have forgiven our debtors. And lead us not into temptation, but deliver us from the evil one.'"

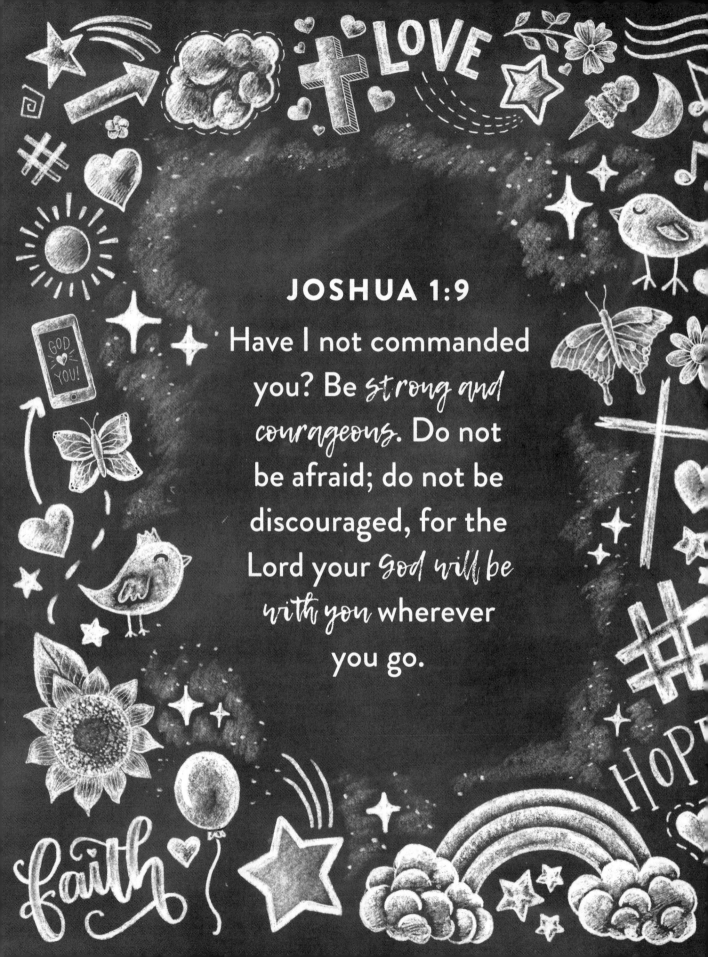

JOSHUA 1:9

Have I not commanded you? Be *strong and courageous*. Do not be afraid; do not be discouraged, for the Lord your *God will be with you* wherever you go.

FEAR

The unknown can be scary. From those jitters you get on the first day of school, to the nerves you get before a big performance or game, it's perfectly natural to feel uncertain and insecure when you're about to embark on something new. But God knew you would experience fear in the face of new things. He calls you to be strong and courageous because He will *never* leave you.

In Scripture, Joshua had big shoes to fill when God called him to succeed Moses in leading the Israelites to the Promised Land. Joshua had witnessed the hardships, trials, and rebellion, as well as the blessings the Israelites encountered as Moses led God's people out of Egypt and wandered in the desert for 40 years looking for the Promised Land. Even though Joshua had been trained by Moses and loved and trusted God, the task was a big one. But God promised to be with Joshua wherever he went, in whatever he did. And He promises the same for you. No matter what path the Lord takes you on in your life, He is always there walking the journey with you. His blessings and reassurances are all around—on beautiful walks in nature, in the promises you hear in worship music and in Scripture, within the friends and loved ones He's surrounded you with, and more. God loves you and He will never leave you, nor forsake you!

Do new things scare you? What new things is God calling you to right now? Share about a time you felt God's presence as you courageously embarked on something new.

_____

_____

_____

_____

_____

_____

_____

_____

_____

_____

_____

_____

_____

_____

_____

_____

Reflection continued . . .

_____
_____
_____
_____
_____
_____
_____
_____
_____
_____
_____
_____
_____
_____
_____
_____
_____
_____
_____
_____
_____
_____
_____
_____
_____
_____
_____
_____
_____
_____
_____
_____
_____
_____
_____

Date

LORD,
thank you

_____
_____
_____
_____
_____
_____
_____
_____
_____
_____
_____
_____
_____
_____
_____
_____
_____
_____

PSALM 34:4

I sought the Lord, and he answered me;
he delivered me from all my fears.

Things on my heart

Highlights

Prayer requests

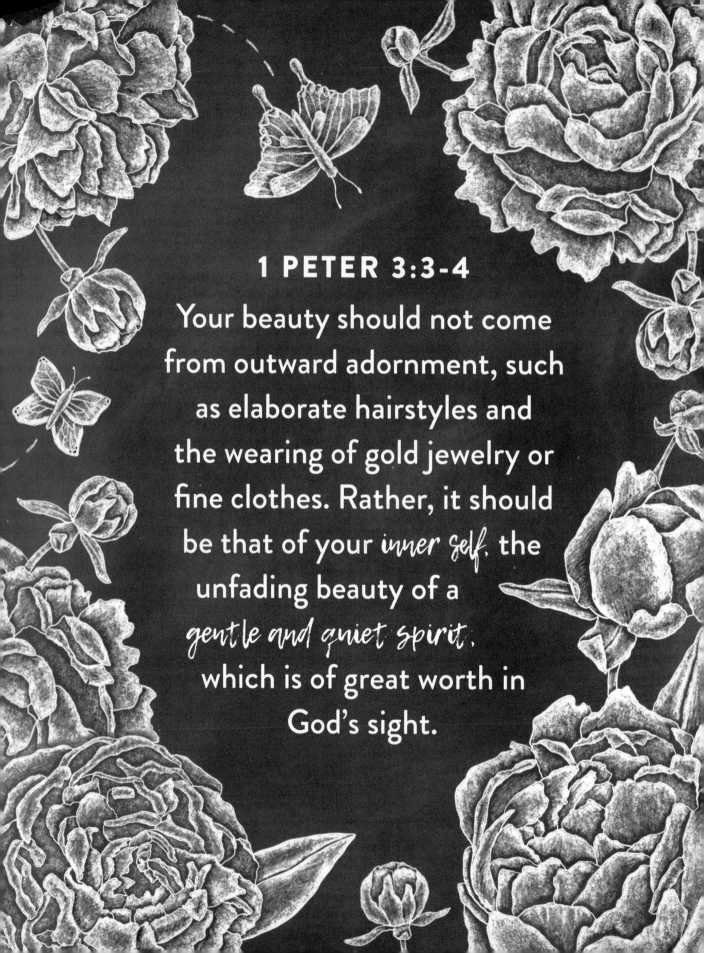

1 PETER 3:3-4

Your beauty should not come from outward adornment, such as elaborate hairstyles and the wearing of gold jewelry or fine clothes. Rather, it should be that of your *inner self*, the unfading beauty of a *gentle and quiet spirit*, which is of great worth in God's sight.

REFLECT

— LOVE & INNER BEAUTY —

What comes to mind when you hear the word *beautiful*? Do you think of that beautiful girl you see in the movies or who you follow on social media? Or maybe you think of that popular girl at school who gets so much attention. All too often, the messages and images sent through social media, television, magazines, and the internet focus solely on what beauty is supposed to *physically* look like.

While the world sends the notion that what matters most is your physical appearance, God is focused on your inner beauty. He looks at your heart (1 Samuel 16:7) and values the beauty of a gentle and quiet spirit, as the verse says on the previous page. Now, does that mean you must be a timid person to be seen as beautiful in God's eyes? Of course not! Scripture is full of God-fearing women who demonstrated humble strength and confidence in who they were. Women like Esther, Ruth, and Mary are just a few examples of women in the Bible who stood up for what was right, but did so with humility and grace. A gentle and quiet spirit aligns with God's character, trusts His plan, and calmly responds to heated situations rather than negatively reacting to them.

Notice the words *unfading beauty* in the verse. Physical beauty fades, but inner beauty lasts, and it can grow as you age! Know that no matter how much pressure you feel to look and dress a certain way, you are a beautiful, precious soul with a purpose that God has planned just for you! Inner beauty radiates from within you into every aspect of your life, and it has no expiration. That's where your truest beauty comes from—from *within*.

What makes someone beautiful to you? Is it how they look and dress, their personality, or a combination of both? How can you filter out the pressure to fit the world's standard of beauty and focus more on God's standard?

_____

_____

_____

_____

_____

_____

_____

_____

Reflection continued . . .

_____
_____
_____
_____
_____
_____
_____
_____
_____
_____
_____
_____
_____
_____
_____
_____
_____
_____
_____
_____
_____
_____
_____
_____
_____
_____
_____
_____
_____
_____
_____
_____
_____
_____
_____
_____
_____
_____
_____
_____

Date

LORD,
thank you

_____
_____
_____
_____
_____
_____
_____
_____
_____
_____
_____
_____
_____
_____
_____
_____
_____
_____
_____
_____
_____
_____

JOHN 15:16

You did not choose me, but I chose you and appointed you so
that you might go and bear fruit—fruit that will last—and so that
whatever you ask in my name the Father will give you.

Things on my heart

_____
_____
_____
_____
_____
_____
_____

Highlights

_____
_____
_____
_____
_____
_____
_____
_____
_____
_____
_____
_____

Prayer requests

_____
_____
_____
_____
_____
_____
_____
_____
_____
_____
_____

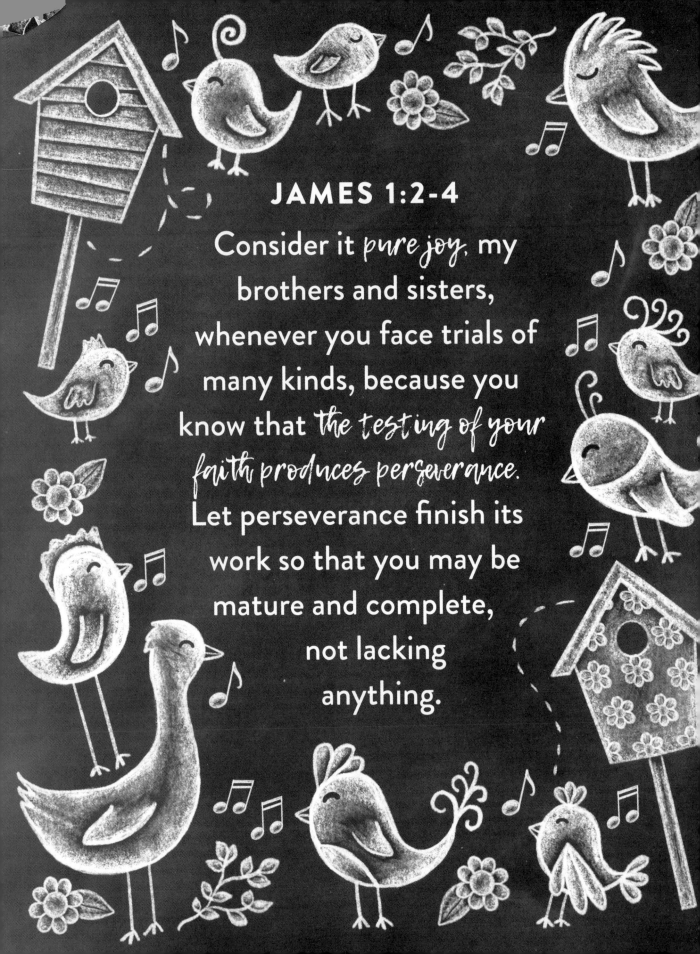

JAMES 1:2-4

Consider it *pure joy,* my brothers and sisters, whenever you face trials of many kinds, because you know that *the testing of your faith produces perseverance.* Let perseverance finish its work so that you may be mature and complete, not lacking anything.

Reflect

ADVERSITY & TRIALS

When you're going through trials and hard times, it can be hard to look at the bigger picture and remember that God is still in control. This is especially hard when you're suffering through something difficult. In Scripture, Joseph (with the coat of many colors) experienced years of family drama, trials, betrayal, adversity, and hard times (Genesis 37-50). He was sold into slavery by his brothers, falsely accused, and thrown into prison for things he didn't do. Yet, regardless of his circumstances, Joseph remained faithful to God and continued to trust His plan. Joseph's perseverance eventually led to him being promoted to second-in-command of Egypt, behind Pharaoh, and he helped save many lives (including his family's) through the dreams God guided him to interpret for others. Now that is something to be joyful about!

No matter what trials or hard times you're enduring or will face in the future, God is with you and still in control. He can use your hardships for your good and the benefit of others, so keep the faith, stand firm, and know that He has a plan and purpose for everything you go through—even the hard stuff. And because God is good (Nahum 1:7), you can trust Him. "Those who know your name trust in you, for you, Lord, have never forsaken those who seek you." (Psalm 9:10).

How do you view trials? Share about a trial you persevered through that had a positive out-come. What did you learn while going through that experience about God and about yourself?

_____

_____

_____

_____

_____

_____

_____

_____

_____

_____

_____

_____

_____

_____

_____

Reflection continued . . .

_____
_____
_____
_____
_____
_____
_____
_____
_____
_____
_____
_____
_____
_____
_____
_____
_____
_____
_____
_____
_____
_____
_____
_____
_____
_____
_____
_____
_____
_____
_____
_____
_____
_____
_____
_____
_____
_____

Date

LORD,
thank you

1 THESSALONIANS 5:16-18

Rejoice always, pray continually, give thanks in all circumstances;
for this is God's will for you in Christ Jesus.

Things on my heart

Highlights

Prayer requests

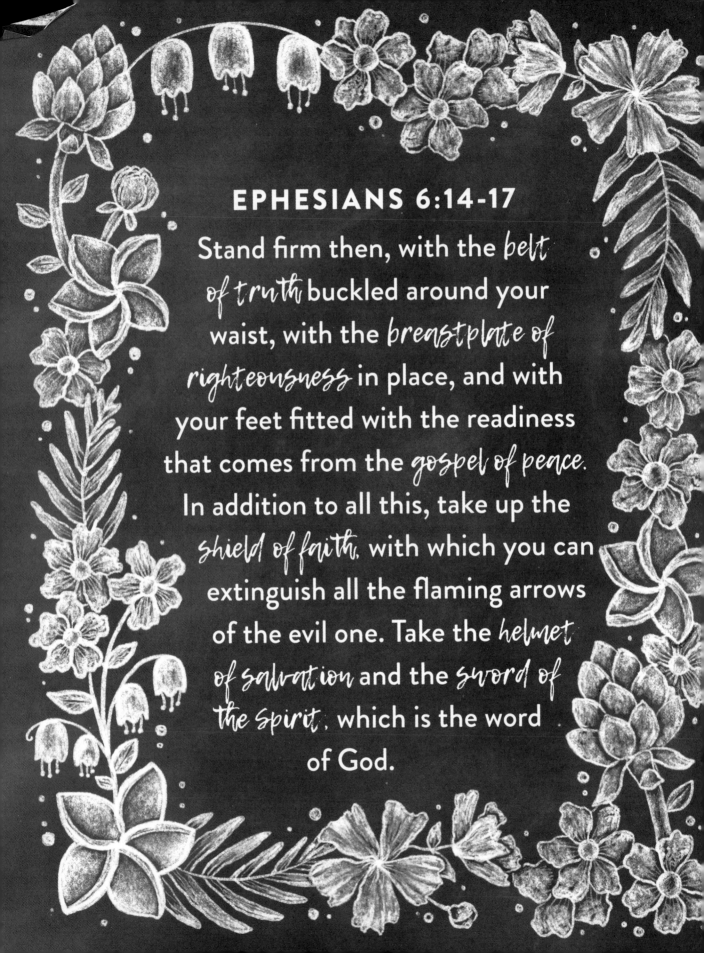

EPHESIANS 6:14-17

Stand firm then, with the *belt of truth* buckled around your waist, with the *breastplate of righteousness* in place, and with your feet fitted with the readiness that comes from the *gospel of peace.* In addition to all this, take up the *shield of faith,* with which you can extinguish all the flaming arrows of the evil one. Take the *helmet of salvation* and the *sword of the Spirit,* which is the word of God.

REFLECT

STRENGTH THROUGH FAITH

In ancient times, protective armor made of bronze, iron, or steel was worn by soldiers in battle. The more covered the soldiers were, the more protected they were. Weapons like swords and bow and arrows had a harder time penetrating skin that was protected, which is why armor wasn't a simple suggestion when it came to battle—it was a literal lifesaving necessity!

In Ephesians, Paul wrote about the importance of putting on our spiritual armor of God. There is a very real spiritual war playing out in our world every day that we can't see. Paul warns us about being able to protect ourselves from these forces of evil and the devil's schemes. He uses the illustration of spiritual armor as a way to protect ourselves, stand firm, and resist temptation.

Each piece of spiritual armor mentioned has a specific role in helping us fight our spiritual battles—the belt of truth, the breastplate of righteousness, the gospel of peace, the shield of faith, the helmet of salvation, and the sword of the Spirit. Notice how five of the six pieces of armor are *defensive*. The sword of the Spirit, which is the Word of God, is both *defensive* and *offensive*. Scripture says that the Word of God is "sharper than a double-edged sword and penetrates even to dividing soul and spirit, joints and marrow" (Hebrews 4:12). Your Bible is your weapon against the enemy! By being rooted in your faith and having God's words written on your heart and in your mind, you can protect yourself and stand firm!

How do you fight your spiritual battles? Which piece of God's armor do you use most when you're enduring trouble? Share about a time you were able to use the armor of God to protect yourself from the enemy's schemes.

Reflection continued . . .

_____

_____

_____

_____

_____

_____

_____

_____

_____

_____

_____

_____

_____

_____

_____

_____

_____

_____

_____

_____

_____

_____

_____

_____

_____

_____

_____

_____

_____

_____

_____

_____

_____

_____

_____

Date

LORD thank you

_____

_____

_____

_____

_____

_____

_____

_____

_____

_____

_____

_____

_____

_____

_____

_____

_____

_____

_____

_____

_____

_____

For the eyes of the Lord are on the righteous and his ears are attentive to their prayer, but the face of the Lord is against those who do evil.

Things on my heart

Highlights

Prayer requests

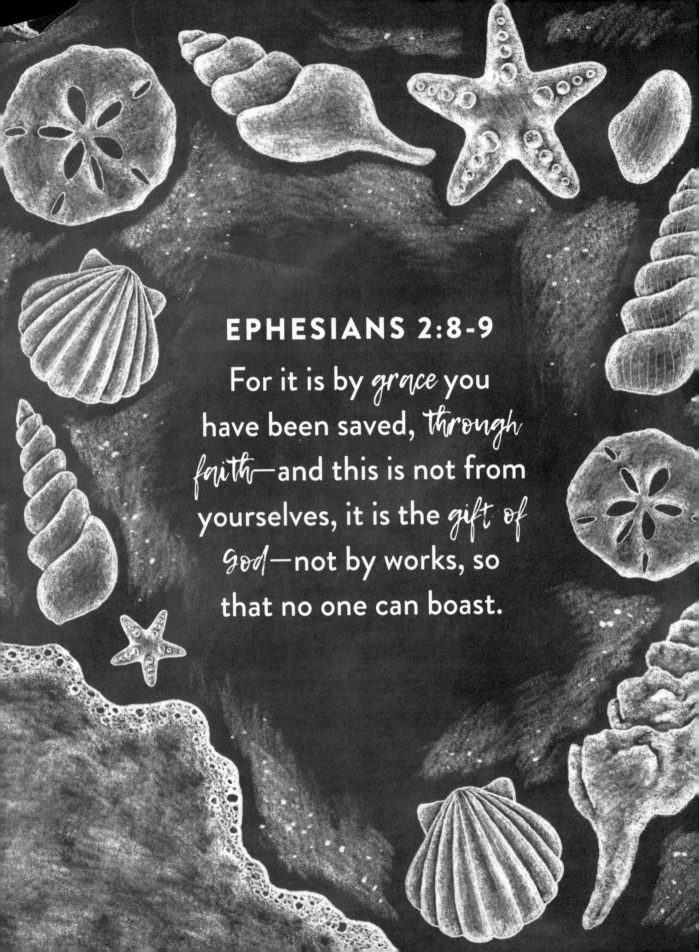

EPHESIANS 2:8-9

For it is by *grace* you have been saved, *through faith*—and this is not from yourselves, it is the *gift of God*—not by works, so that no one can boast.

GRACE & FORGIVENESS

A lot of things in life are earned. You study hard for an exam, so you can pass and earn a good grade. You practice for your sport, so you can improve and win games. You work at your job, so you can earn money to buy things. The list goes on and on. Fortunately, your salvation does *not* work this way. There is nothing you can do to *earn* your salvation. It is the *free gift* of God (Romans 3:22-24, Romans 5:12-21, Romans 6:23)!

When God sent His Son, Jesus Christ, to die on the cross, His death paid the penalty for our sins and His resurrection conquered death. Because of our sins, death is our ultimate punishment, but because of Jesus's sacrifice, we are offered the free gift of eternal life through Him. This is where your salvation comes from! The same power that raised Christ from the dead dwells within you when you believe, have faith, and accept Jesus as your Savior (Romans 8:11)! "For God so loved the world, that He gave his one and only Son, that whoever believes in him will not perish but have eternal life" (John 3:16).

Have you ever felt that you had to earn God's favor? If so, share about that experience and how you felt in that moment. How does this verse encourage you knowing that by God's grace you have been saved through faith and not because of anything you do to earn it?

_____
_____
_____
_____
_____
_____
_____
_____
_____
_____
_____
_____
_____
_____
_____
_____

Reflection continued . . .

_____
_____
_____
_____
_____
_____
_____
_____
_____
_____
_____
_____
_____
_____
_____
_____
_____
_____
_____
_____
_____
_____
_____
_____
_____
_____
_____
_____
_____
_____
_____
_____
_____
_____

Date

LORD,
thank you

_____
_____
_____
_____
_____
_____
_____
_____
_____
_____
_____
_____
_____
_____
_____
_____
_____
_____
_____
_____

LUKE 11:13

If you then, though you are evil, know how to give good gifts to your
children, how much more will your Father in heaven give the Holy
Spirit to those who ask him!

Things on my heart

_____
_____
_____
_____
_____
_____
_____
_____

Highlights

_____
_____
_____
_____
_____
_____
_____
_____
_____
_____
_____
_____

Prayer requests

_____
_____
_____
_____
_____
_____
_____
_____
_____
_____
_____
_____

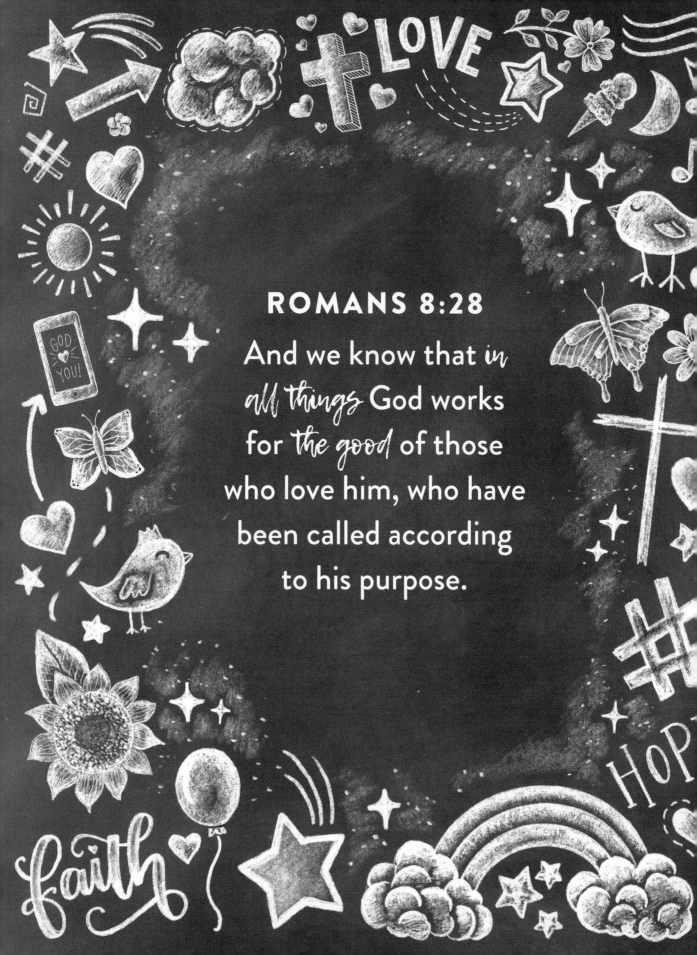

ROMANS 8:28

And we know that *in all things* God works for *the good* of those who love him, who have been called according to his purpose.

AWE & SOVEREIGNTY

In all things, God works for your good. "All things" encompasses everything—the good, the bad, and the things in between. In the Old Testament, when Joseph was enduring trial after trial, he couldn't see past his present circumstances, but God could! From his brothers' betrayal to being falsely accused and thrown into prison, God used this series of hardships to ultimately lead Joseph in saving his people and the land of Egypt from the famine. What was intended to harm Joseph, God used for good (Genesis 50:20)! How encouraging is that?

While life is filled with ups and downs, remember that God is sovereign and still in control. He can use the events in your life (yes, even the difficult ones) for your good and His glory. Just like in the story of Joseph, God can see beyond your current circumstances, beyond the tough things you're going through, the mistakes you've made, and the hurt you have felt. He knows what's ahead, sees the bigger picture, and you can trust Him to lead you. Scripture says to "Trust in the Lord with all your heart, and lean not on your own understanding. In all your ways submit to him, and he will make your paths straight" (Proverbs 3:5-6).

Has there ever been a time you were able to look back at a series of events from your past and see how God worked them together for good? If so, what happened? How does this verse encourage you going forward through the hurdles and bumps of life, knowing that God is sovereign and works out all things for your good?

_____

_____

_____

_____

_____

_____

_____

_____

_____

_____

_____

_____

_____

_____

Reflection continued . . .

_____
_____
_____
_____
_____
_____
_____
_____
_____
_____
_____
_____
_____
_____
_____
_____
_____
_____
_____
_____
_____
_____
_____
_____
_____
_____
_____
_____
_____
_____
_____
_____
_____
_____
_____
_____
_____
_____
_____
_____

Date

LORD,
thank you

This is the confidence we have in approaching God; that if we ask anything according to his will, he hears us.

Things on my heart

_____
_____
_____
_____
_____

Highlights

_____
_____
_____
_____
_____
_____
_____
_____
_____

Prayer requests

_____
_____
_____
_____
_____
_____
_____
_____
_____

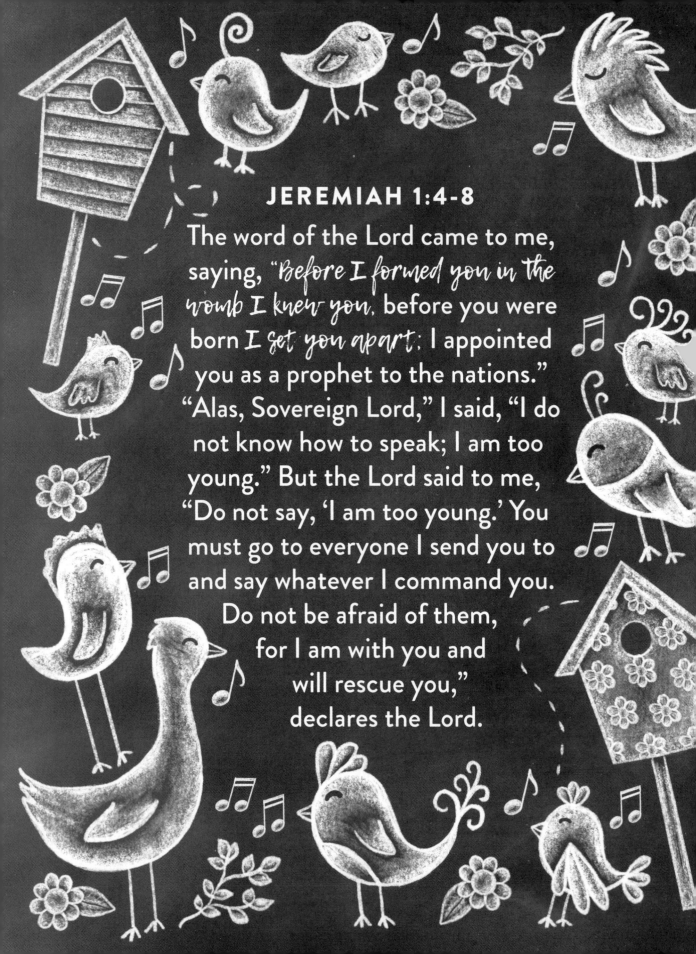

JEREMIAH 1:4-8

The word of the Lord came to me, saying, "*Before I formed you in the womb I knew you,* before you were born *I set you apart;* I appointed you as a prophet to the nations." "Alas, Sovereign Lord," I said, "I do not know how to speak; I am too young." But the Lord said to me, "Do not say, 'I am too young.' You must go to everyone I send you to and say whatever I command you. Do not be afraid of them, for I am with you and will rescue you," declares the Lord.

PROVISION & FAITHFULNESS

Jeremiah was a prophet of the Lord. He is called the "weeping prophet" because of the anguish and grief he felt as he delivered God's message of judgment to his people for their rebellious ways. Jeremiah was young, inexperienced, and doubted himself. He was unsure of how to speak to God's people in a meaningful way, and felt that his young age would be a hindrance to his success (Jeremiah 1:6). However, God saw past Jeremiah's youth and insecurities, and knew that he was the perfect guy for the task at hand. God promised to be with Jeremiah, to speak through him, and to protect him in whatever resistance he faced (Jeremiah 1:8, Jeremiah 1:19).

God had a special plan for Jeremiah's life, and He has a special plan for you! You were created on purpose *for a purpose*. Whenever you feel unsure of yourself and your abilities, remember that God is with you. When God calls you to something, He will equip you with all that you need, and qualify you for the job regardless of your age and experience. "The Lord is my strength and my shield; my heart trusts in him, and he helps me. My heart leaps for joy, and with my song I praise him" (Psalm 28:7).

What insecurities do you struggle with? Do you ever doubt your abilities? How does this verse encourage you, knowing that God can still use you for His perfect purpose regardless of your age, experience, or insecurities?

_____

_____

_____

_____

_____

_____

_____

_____

_____

_____

_____

_____

_____

_____

_____

_____

_____

Reflection continued . . .

LORD
thank you

JAMES 1:5-6

If any of you lacks wisdom, you should ask God, who gives generously to all without finding fault, and it will be given to you. But when you ask, you must believe and not doubt, because the one who doubts is like a wave of the sea, blown and tossed by the wind.

Things on my heart

Highlights

Prayer requests

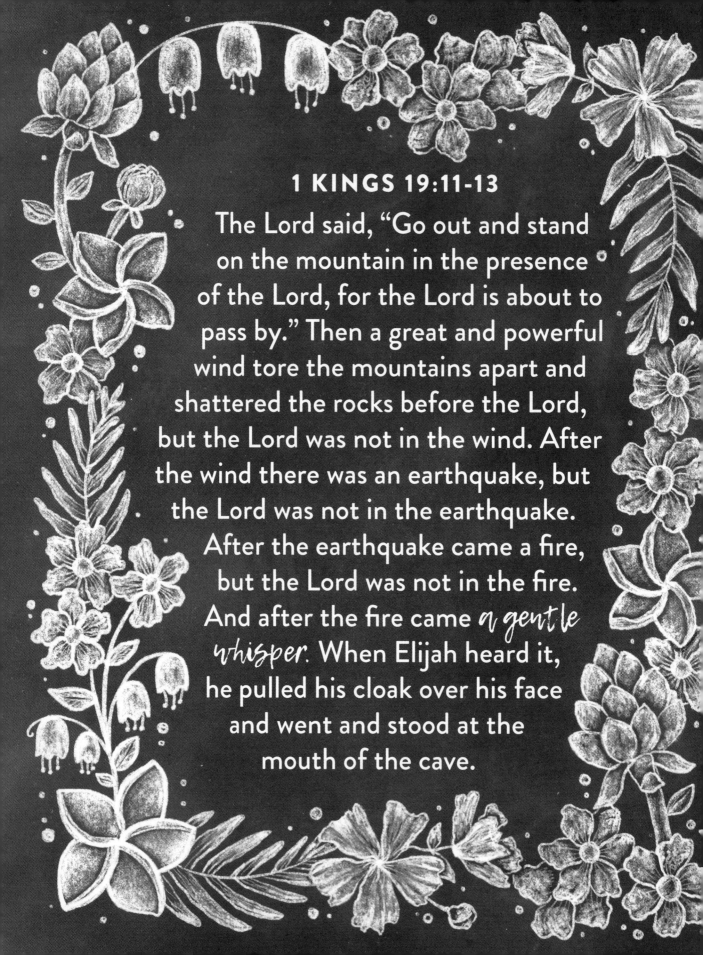

1 KINGS 19:11-13

The Lord said, "Go out and stand on the mountain in the presence of the Lord, for the Lord is about to pass by." Then a great and powerful wind tore the mountains apart and shattered the rocks before the Lord, but the Lord was not in the wind. After the wind there was an earthquake, but the Lord was not in the earthquake. After the earthquake came a fire, but the Lord was not in the fire. And after the fire came *a gentle whisper.* When Elijah heard it, he pulled his cloak over his face and went and stood at the mouth of the cave.

GOD'S LOVE

The message from these verses is quite significant. Elijah is hiding in a cave, fearing for his life, when the Lord tells him to go out and stand on the mountain in the presence of the Lord, for He is about to pass by. Elijah waits as a powerful wind, an earthquake, and a fire appear, one after the other. But the Lord was not in those. Then there's a *gentle whisper*. At hearing this, Elijah gets up and goes out, knowing it's the Lord.

Sometimes, we get so wrapped up in our day-to-day busy lives that we forget to pause, be still, and listen for God's gentle voice speaking to us. You've got a packed schedule of school, practice, homework, chores, events, and the list goes on. This constant state of busyness, while good at times, can also distract you from hearing God's sweet, intimate whispers. This is why it's so important to be intentional about your quiet time with God. Whispers are meant for those within close proximity who are listening. This speaks volumes about who God is. He's nearby—close enough that He can speak to you in a gentle whisper! As Scripture says, "Be still before the Lord, and wait patiently for him..." (Psalm 37:7).

Share about a time you felt that God was speaking to you. What happened? How can you be more intentional about quieting the noise and listening for God's sweet, gentle whispers?

_____

_____

_____

_____

_____

_____

_____

_____

_____

_____

_____

_____

_____

_____

Reflection continued . . .

_____
_____
_____
_____
_____
_____
_____
_____
_____
_____
_____
_____
_____
_____
_____
_____
_____
_____
_____
_____
_____
_____
_____
_____
_____
_____
_____
_____
_____
_____
_____
_____
_____
_____
_____
_____
_____
_____
_____

Date

LORD thank you

_____
_____
_____
_____
_____
_____
_____
_____
_____
_____
_____
_____
_____
_____
_____
_____
_____
_____
_____
_____
_____
_____

EZRA 8:23

So we fasted and petitioned our God about this,
and he answered our prayer.

Things on my heart

Highlights

Prayer requests

ISAIAH 41:10

So do not fear, for I am with you; do not be dismayed, for I am your God. I will strengthen you and help you; I will uphold you with my righteous right hand.

FEER

Anxiety and fear are nothing new. The Bible is full of people who were fearful of what God was asking them to do. For example, look at Moses. He was chosen by God to deliver the Israelites from captivity in Egypt. When God revealed His plan to use Moses to free the Israelites, Moses responded with fear and doubt in himself and even asked God to send someone else (Exodus 4:10-13)! Regardless, God gave Moses the strength he needed, despite his fears and insecurities, to accomplish God's will in saving the Israelites.

Whatever fears you're struggling with right now, God is still with you. Fear is nothing He can't handle, so give your struggles, doubts, and insecurities to God, the creator of you, who knows you better than you know yourself. By praying and/or journaling the things on your heart to Him, you release yourself from carrying your burdens alone. He hears you and He cares (Psalm 55:22, 1 Peter 5:6-7). Scripture says He created your inmost being and knit you together in your mother's womb (Psalm 139:13). That is how intimately involved He is with the details of your life. He knows your fears and the struggles you face, and He will give you the strength you need.

What things make you feel fearful? How do you cope when you are feeling anxious and afraid? Share about a time you felt God's strength and peace through a difficult time.

_____

_____

_____

_____

_____

_____

_____

_____

_____

_____

_____

_____

_____

_____

_____

_____

_____

Reflection continued . . .

Date

LORD,
thank you

PSALM 18:6

In my distress I called to the Lord; I cried to my God for help. From
his temple he heard my voice; my cry came before him, into his ears.

Things on my heart

Highlights

Prayer requests

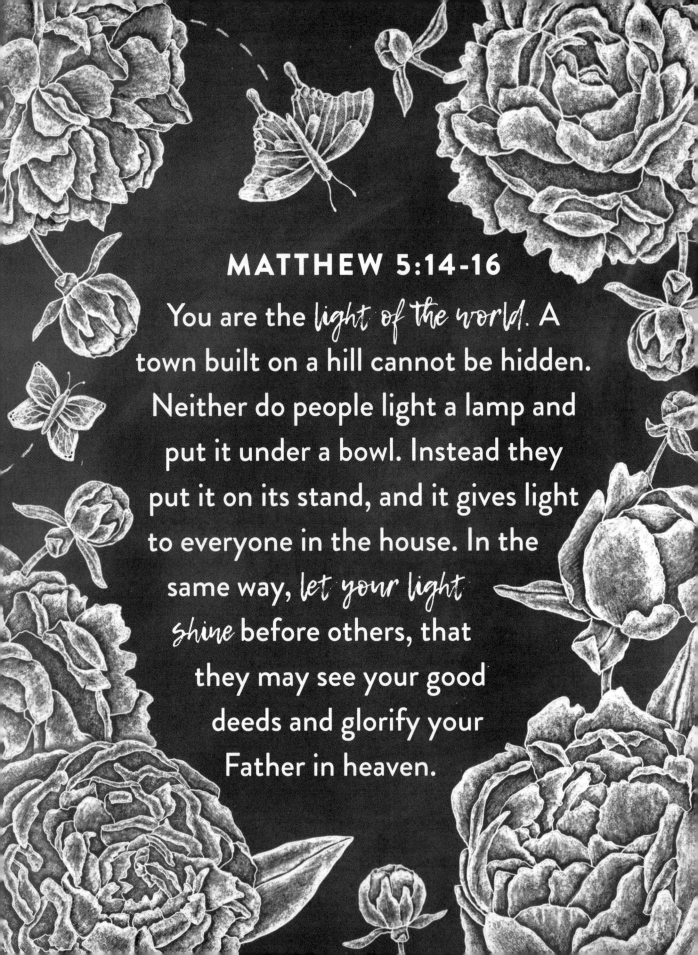

MATTHEW 5:14-16

You are the *light of the world.* A town built on a hill cannot be hidden. Neither do people light a lamp and put it under a bowl. Instead they put it on its stand, and it gives light to everyone in the house. In the same way, *let your light shine* before others, that they may see your good deeds and glorify your Father in heaven.

REFLECT

LOVE & INNER BEAUTY

Have you ever been on the outskirts of a city at night? It's hard not to notice the radiant amount of light coming from it. It's captivating and bright. It stands out among the darkness of the night and people are drawn to its beauty. In the same way, you are the light of the world! When you became a Christian and accepted Jesus as your Savior, you were set apart and filled with the Holy Spirit (Ephesians 1:13-14).

You have a hope inside you that people are so desperately searching for, and by shining your light for others to see, you can gently point them toward God. Your actions, words, deeds, and how you love others (while imperfect, you are human!) should reflect the inner workings of your salvation. The community you live in, the school you attend, and the team(s) you play for are all part of the mission field God has placed you in. So let your light shine and watch how God moves!

In what ways are you letting your light shine to others? Has anyone ever told you they noticed something different about you, and about how you live your life? What does this verse mean to you?

_____
_____
_____
_____
_____
_____
_____
_____
_____
_____
_____
_____
_____
_____
_____
_____
_____
_____
_____
_____
_____

Reflection continued . . .

_____
_____
_____
_____
_____
_____
_____
_____
_____
_____
_____
_____
_____
_____
_____
_____
_____
_____
_____
_____
_____
_____
_____
_____
_____
_____
_____
_____
_____
_____
_____
_____
_____
_____
_____
_____
_____
_____
_____
_____

Date

LORD,
thank you

_____
_____
_____
_____
_____
_____
_____
_____
_____
_____
_____
_____
_____
_____
_____
_____
_____
_____
_____
_____
_____

ACTS 4:31

After they prayed, the place where they were meeting was shaken.
And they were all filled with the Holy Spirit and spoke the word
of God boldly.

Things on my heart

_____
_____
_____
_____
_____
_____

Highlights

_____
_____
_____
_____
_____
_____
_____
_____
_____
_____
_____

Prayer requests

_____
_____
_____
_____
_____
_____
_____
_____
_____
_____
_____

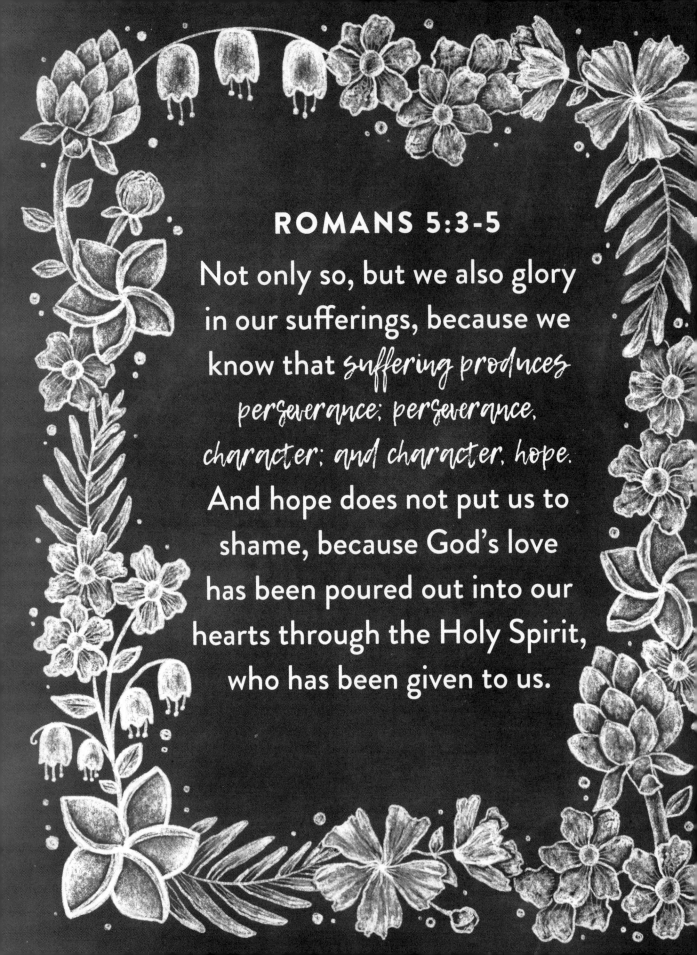

ROMANS 5:3-5

Not only so, but we also glory in our sufferings, because we know that *suffering produces perseverance; perseverance, character; and character, hope.* And hope does not put us to shame, because God's love has been poured out into our hearts through the Holy Spirit, who has been given to us.

ADVERSITY & TRIALS

Suffering is difficult. Being a Christian doesn't prevent us from going through difficult times, but it does give us greater perspective. And, oftentimes, there's a rainbow waiting for us at the end of the storm. As a Christian, you know that God is in control, and everything you face must first go through Him and His sovereignty. He has a plan and a purpose for all of it, and He promises to work all things out for your good (Romans 8:28)!

When you are experiencing adversity and suffering, God is still at work. He uses these experiences to shape your character and heart, and oftentimes, going through trials draws you closer to Him and His loving, outstretched arms! Through the Holy Spirit, you can walk through life's trials with greater confidence knowing that God sees you, understands completely, and is involved.

Share about a trial you went through that changed your character and perspective. How can you approach life's trials with confidence, knowing that God walks with you through everything you encounter?

_____
_____
_____
_____
_____
_____
_____
_____
_____
_____
_____
_____
_____
_____
_____
_____
_____
_____
_____

Reflection continued . . .

LORD, thank you

ROMANS 12:12

Be joyful in hope, patient in affliction, faithful in prayer.

Things on my heart

Highlights

Prayer requests

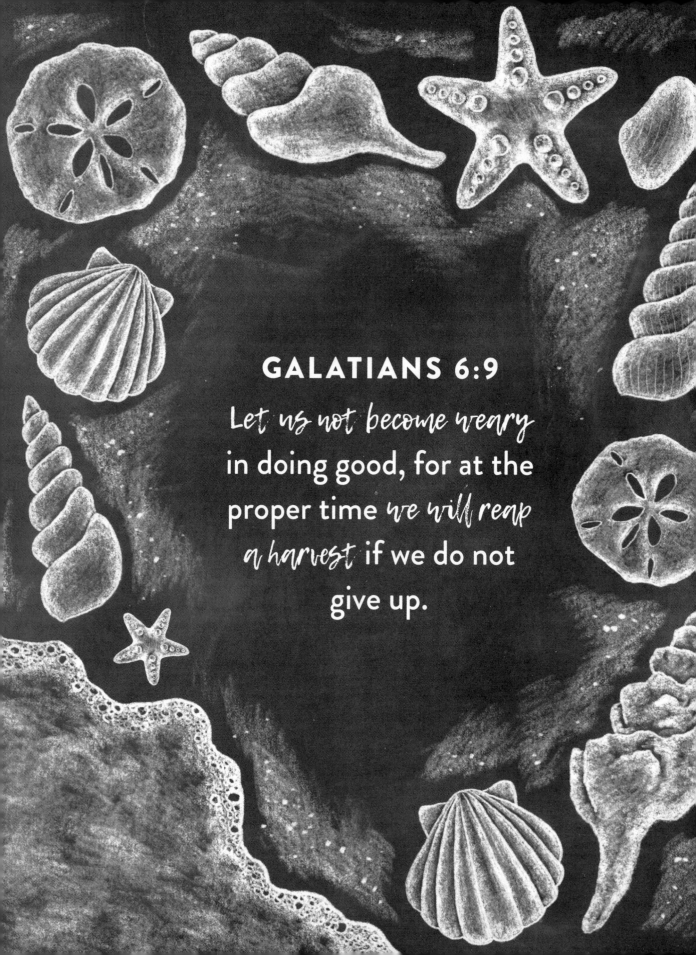

GALATIANS 6:9

Let us not become weary in doing good, for at the proper time we will reap a harvest if we do not give up.

REFLECT

STRENGTH THROUGH FAITH

Has being a Christian ever felt tiresome or difficult for you? Paul gives us an agricultural analogy in Galatians 6:7-8: "Do not be deceived: God cannot be mocked. A man reaps what he sows. Whoever sows to please their flesh, from the flesh will reap destruction; whoever sows to please the Spirit, from the Spirit will reap eternal life." When a farmer sows wisely, he yields a bountiful crop. When he sows poorly, he yields a weak crop, if any at all. A bountiful harvest is the result of a farmer's intentional planning, time, effort, and care. It requires patience and hope that everything he's working for *now* will yield a harvest *later* at the proper time. During the planting season, the farmer does not know which seeds will go on to produce a harvest. But he sees the bigger picture, trusts the process, and plants the seeds accordingly.

You are similar to a farmer, but in the spiritual sense. As a Christian, you have a calling to live your life for God. You are constantly "planting seeds" everywhere you go—in your neighborhood, at your school, your job, and the teams you play for. Your actions, your attitude, your behavior, and the way you live your life sends messages to others. You may never know which "seeds" you plant will go on to produce a harvest, but like the farmer, you can still plant them and leave their future in God's hands. Like a tired farmer working through difficult terrain, there will be times the Christian life is hard and tiresome. But you have hope because of Jesus, and a bountiful harvest waiting for you in eternity (1 Corinthians 3:13-15, 2 Corinthians 5:10, Revelation 22:12).

How can you keep your eyes on God when you feel tired or weary in your Christian walk? Where in your life's activities are you "planting seeds" and allowing others to observe your actions, attitude, and behavior? How does this verse encourage you?

_____

_____

_____

_____

_____

_____

_____

_____

_____

_____

_____

Reflection continued . . .

Date

LORD
thank you

PSALM 40:1

I waited patiently for the Lord; he turned to me and heard my cry.

Things on my heart

Highlights

Prayer requests

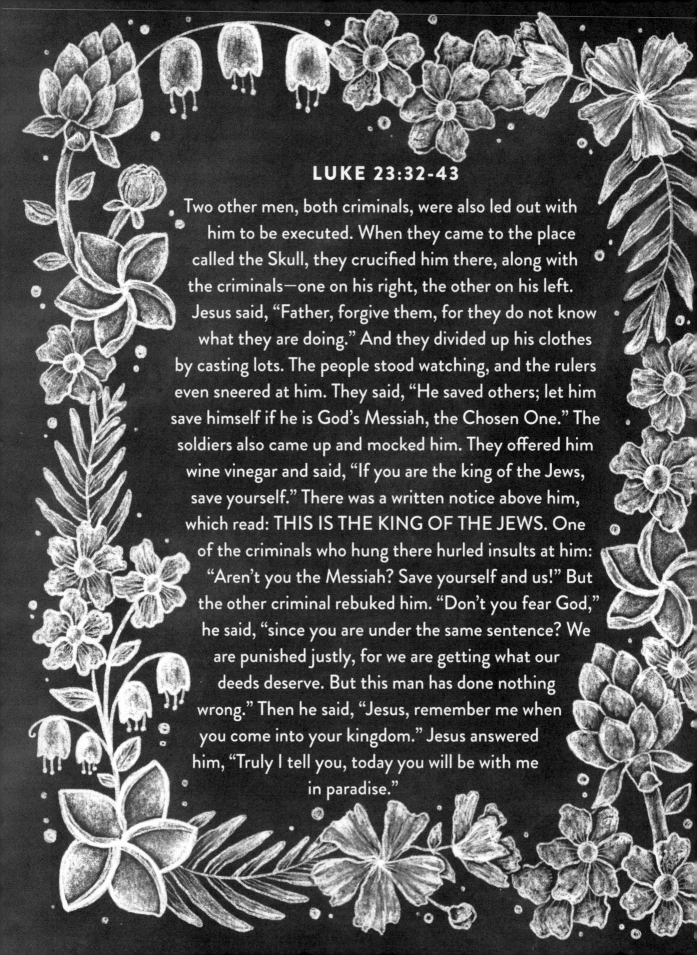

LUKE 23:32-43

Two other men, both criminals, were also led out with him to be executed. When they came to the place called the Skull, they crucified him there, along with the criminals—one on his right, the other on his left. Jesus said, "Father, forgive them, for they do not know what they are doing." And they divided up his clothes by casting lots. The people stood watching, and the rulers even sneered at him. They said, "He saved others; let him save himself if he is God's Messiah, the Chosen One." The soldiers also came up and mocked him. They offered him wine vinegar and said, "If you are the king of the Jews, save yourself." There was a written notice above him, which read: THIS IS THE KING OF THE JEWS. One of the criminals who hung there hurled insults at him: "Aren't you the Messiah? Save yourself and us!" But the other criminal rebuked him. "Don't you fear God," he said, "since you are under the same sentence? We are punished justly, for we are getting what our deeds deserve. But this man has done nothing wrong." Then he said, "Jesus, remember me when you come into your kingdom." Jesus answered him, "Truly I tell you, today you will be with me in paradise."

GRACE & FORGIVENESS

When Jesus was nailed to the cross to be crucified, two criminals were crucified on crosses next to Him for crimes they committed. There is a vast difference between these two criminals. One threw insults at Jesus while the other displayed humility and asked Jesus to remember him in heaven. Jesus, full of kindness and compassion (even while nailed to a cross!) not only responded with grace, but also guaranteed this man a place in heaven. How incredible is that?

God is merciful and forgiving, seeing past your exterior and into the very core of your heart. He knows you at the deepest level and He knows when you are truly grieved and repentant for your sins. No matter what sins you've committed in your past, or the shame that burdens you, it is never too late to turn to God. 1 John 1:9 says, "If we confess our sins, he is faithful and just and will forgive us our sins and purify us from all unrighteousness." This is why Jesus came! His death and resurrection conquered death and the consequences of sin so that through your faith and acceptance of Him, your sins are no longer counted against you (2 Corinthians 5:17-19). Share your heart with Him, pray to Him, and give Him your burdens. He loves you and He cares (Psalm 103:11-12).

Do you believe that God is merciful and forgiving? Have you confessed your sins to Him and given Him the reins to lead your life? How do these verses encourage you, knowing that through Jesus, you are set free from your sins (Acts 13:38-39)?

_____
_____
_____
_____
_____
_____
_____
_____
_____
_____
_____
_____
_____
_____
_____
_____

Reflection continued . . .

_____
_____
_____
_____
_____
_____
_____
_____
_____
_____
_____
_____
_____
_____
_____
_____
_____
_____
_____
_____
_____
_____
_____
_____
_____
_____
_____
_____
_____
_____
_____
_____
_____
_____
_____
_____
_____
_____
_____

Date

LORD,
thank you

2 CHRONICLES 7:14

...if my people, who are called by my name, will humble themselves and pray and seek my face and turn from their wicked ways, then I will hear from heaven, and I will forgive their sin and will heal their land.

Things on my heart

_____
_____
_____
_____
_____
_____
_____

Highlights

_____
_____
_____
_____
_____
_____
_____
_____
_____
_____
_____
_____

Prayer requests

_____
_____
_____
_____
_____
_____
_____
_____
_____
_____
_____
_____

EPHESIANS 2:10

For we are *God's handiwork*, created in Christ Jesus to do *good works*, which God prepared in advance for us to do.

—— AWE & SOVEREIGNTY ——

In Scripture, Jesus often spoke in parables—stories with a lesson. One was the parable of the talents in Matthew 25:14-30. In this story, a master is going on a journey, but first gives three of his servants different amounts of talents (bags of gold) to care for while he is away. To the first servant, he gives five bags. To the second servant, he gives two bags. The third servant received one bag. This was intentional as the master gave a specific amount of wealth to each servant *according to his ability*.

After a time, the master returned to settle accounts with each servant. The first two servants used what the master gave them and doubled what they were given. The third servant hid his bag of gold in the ground and did nothing with it. In the end, the third servant is stripped of the one bag of gold the master entrusted him with, while the first two are rewarded for investing what was given to them.

You are God's masterpiece; a unique, beautiful soul in a body that is exclusively yours and given to you by God. In a world of over seven billion people, there is *no one exactly like you*! Think about that—you are the *original you*, and you were created with *a purpose*! The talents and abilities you have that come so easily to you are not an accident—God has entrusted them to you. It is up to you to use them. Using the gifts God has blessed you with glorifies Him and can serve as a blessing to others in the process.

What unique talents and abilities has God blessed you with? Does anything hold you back from using your abilities? How are you using and growing your talents to glorify God and serve others?

_____

_____

_____

_____

_____

_____

_____

_____

_____

_____

_____

_____

Reflection continued . . .

_____
_____
_____
_____
_____
_____
_____
_____
_____
_____
_____
_____
_____
_____
_____
_____
_____
_____
_____
_____
_____
_____
_____
_____
_____
_____
_____
_____
_____
_____
_____
_____
_____
_____
_____
_____

Date

LORD,
thank you

_____
_____
_____
_____
_____
_____
_____
_____
_____
_____
_____
_____
_____
_____
_____
_____
_____
_____
_____
_____
_____
_____
_____
_____
_____

For there is no difference between Jew and Gentile—the same Lord is Lord of all and richly blesses all who call on him, for, "Everyone who calls on the name of the Lord will be saved."

Things on my heart

Highlights

Prayer requests

1 CORINTHIANS 10:13

No temptation has overtaken you except what is common to mankind. And *God is faithful*, he will not let you be tempted beyond what you can bear. But when you are tempted, *he will also provide a way out* so that you can endure it.

PROVISION & FAITHFULNESS

We live in an imperfect world where the enemy lurks and seeks to destroy. Temptations are all around and no one is immune to them. This is why it's so important to choose your friends wisely, and to protect yourself from situations that can lead to bad outcomes. Jesus Himself was tempted by the devil (Matthew 4:1-11). But though He was tempted, He resisted and overcame. He stood firm in what He knew to be true, *responded with Scripture*, and the devil fled. God's Word is described as being the sword of the Spirit and sharper than a double-edged sword (Ephesians 6:17, Hebrews 4:12). It's no wonder, then, that Jesus used the truth of Scripture to stand firm and resist temptation.

You, too, can overcome any temptation that comes your way. James 4:7 says to, "Submit yourselves, then, to God. Resist the devil and he will flee from you." You are a child of God and the power of the Holy Spirit lives in you! When you are facing temptation, pray to God and ask Him to help you. He will give you the strength and stamina you need to stand firm, turn away, and overcome.

What do you do when you are faced with temptation? Do you turn to God for help? Share about a time when you resisted temptation and how you overcame it.

_____

_____

_____

_____

_____

_____

_____

_____

_____

_____

_____

_____

_____

_____

_____

_____

Reflection continued . . .

_____
_____
_____
_____
_____
_____
_____
_____
_____
_____
_____
_____
_____
_____
_____
_____
_____
_____
_____
_____
_____
_____
_____
_____
_____
_____
_____
_____
_____
_____
_____
_____
_____
_____

Date

LORD,
thank you

MATTHEW 26:41

"Watch and pray so that you will not fall into temptation.
The spirit is willing, but the flesh is weak."

Things on my heart

Highlights

Prayer requests

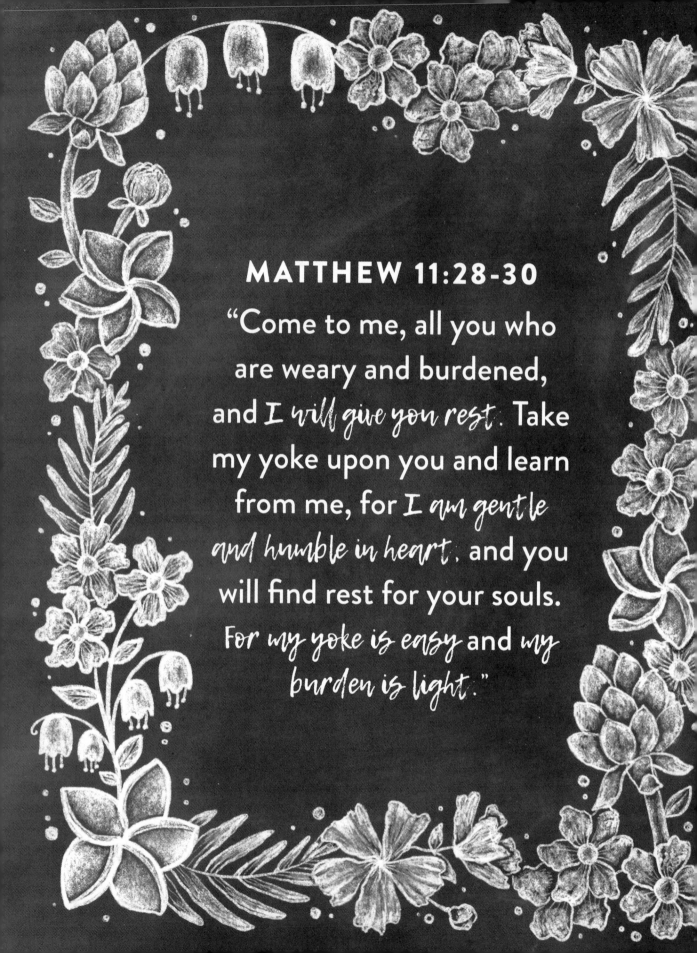

MATTHEW 11:28-30

"Come to me, all you who are weary and burdened, and I will give you rest. Take my yoke upon you and learn from me, for I am gentle and humble in heart, and you will find rest for your souls. For my yoke is easy and my burden is light."

REFLECT

GOD'S LOVE

When you hear the word *yoke*, you may picture a "yolk," which is the yellow part of an egg. But a yoke is actually a strong, horizontal wooden bar with straps that holds two animals side-by-side. The bar sits atop the two animals, such as oxen, trained to pull heavy loads. Once the yoke is attached to the animals, they work side-by-side to pull whatever load they're hauling. Historically, when a young ox needed training, it could be yoked with a stronger, more experienced ox that could lead and train it in the way it should go. By submitting to the trained, more experienced ox, the young ox could learn how to haul the load.

In the same way, Jesus encourages you to take His yoke upon you and learn from Him! He is gentle and humble in heart, and He will bear the weight of your troubles. The heavy burdens and hardships of living in a fallen world can be tiresome and overwhelming. But with Jesus by your side, carrying your load with you, you can find rest. We have a loving God who invites us to walk life's journey with Him. Talk to Him, share your heart and your burdens with Him, and let Him carry you through.

How do you respond when you face hardship? Have you ever experienced God carrying you through tough times? What was it like? What does this verse mean to you?

_____

_____

_____

_____

_____

_____

_____

_____

_____

_____

_____

_____

_____

_____

_____

_____

_____

Reflection continued . . .

Date

LORD,
thank you

PSALM 34:17

The righteous cry out, and the Lord hears them;
he delivers them from all their troubles.

Things on my heart

Highlights

Prayer requests

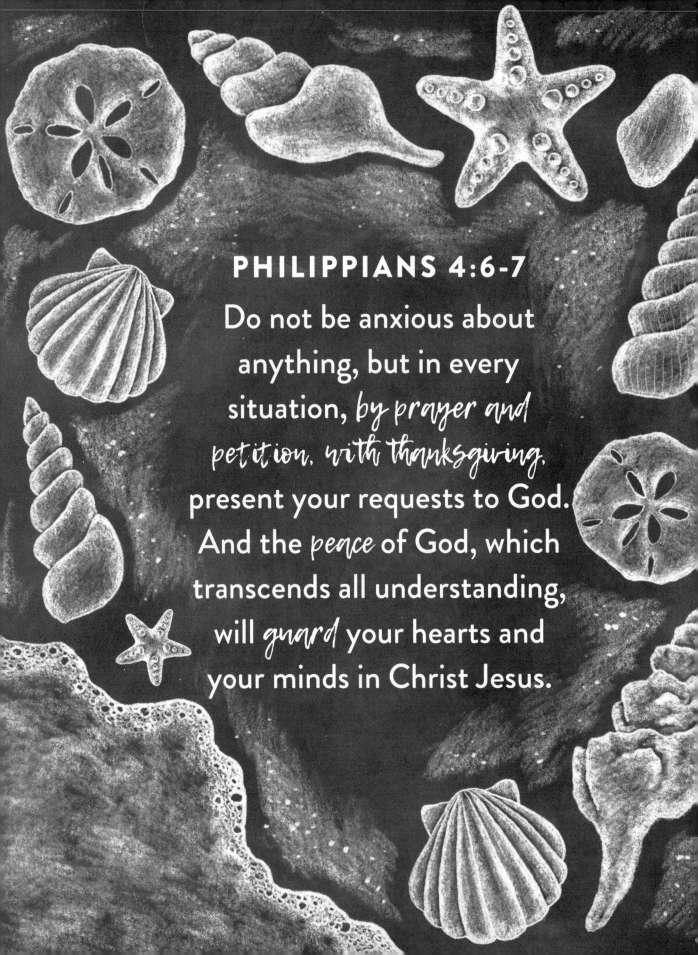

PHILIPPIANS 4:6-7

Do not be anxious about anything, but in every situation, *by prayer and petition, with thanksgiving,* present your requests to God. And the *peace* of God, which transcends all understanding, will *guard* your hearts and your minds in Christ Jesus.

FEAR

Scripture is full of people who prayed to God in their distress. One was a king named Hezekiah who did what was right in God's eyes. He honored God with his choices and trusted in Him. During his reign, Hezekiah became very ill, to the point of death. Isaiah, a prophet from God, told Hezekiah he would die from this illness. Could you imagine the fear and anxiety Hezekiah must have felt upon hearing this? Rather than wallow in self-pity, Scripture says that Hezekiah turned to the wall *and prayed* (2 Kings 20:2-4). He talked to God, reminding Him of his love and devotion to Him, and he wept bitterly in the process. Scripture says that Isaiah returned after this. He shared that God had heard Hezekiah's prayer and would heal him, granting him fifteen more years of life!

There is power in prayer. As seen in the story of King Hezekiah, God hears your prayers and sees your tears! When you are anxious and afraid, give your worries to God. He is your refuge and strength (Psalm 46:1). Talk to Him, cry to Him, and share your struggles with Him. He is always there for you and will never leave you (Deuteronomy 31:8). We can find peace in knowing that God is sovereign and in control regardless of the circumstances. He loves you and has a plan for everything you go through, even the hard stuff.

Have you ever experienced fear as a result of an injury or illness? If so, what happened? How does this verse encourage you, knowing that God hears your prayers, wants to hear from you, and gives you His peace?

_____

_____

_____

_____

_____

_____

_____

_____

_____

_____

_____

_____

_____

_____

Reflection continued . . .

Date

LORD
thank you

Is anyone among you sick? Let them call the elders of the church to pray over them and anoint them with oil in the name of the Lord. And the prayer offered in faith will make the sick person well; the Lord will raise them up. If they have sinned, they will be forgiven.

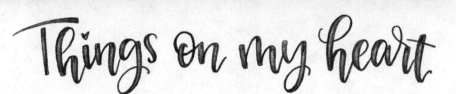

Things on my heart

Highlights

Prayer requests

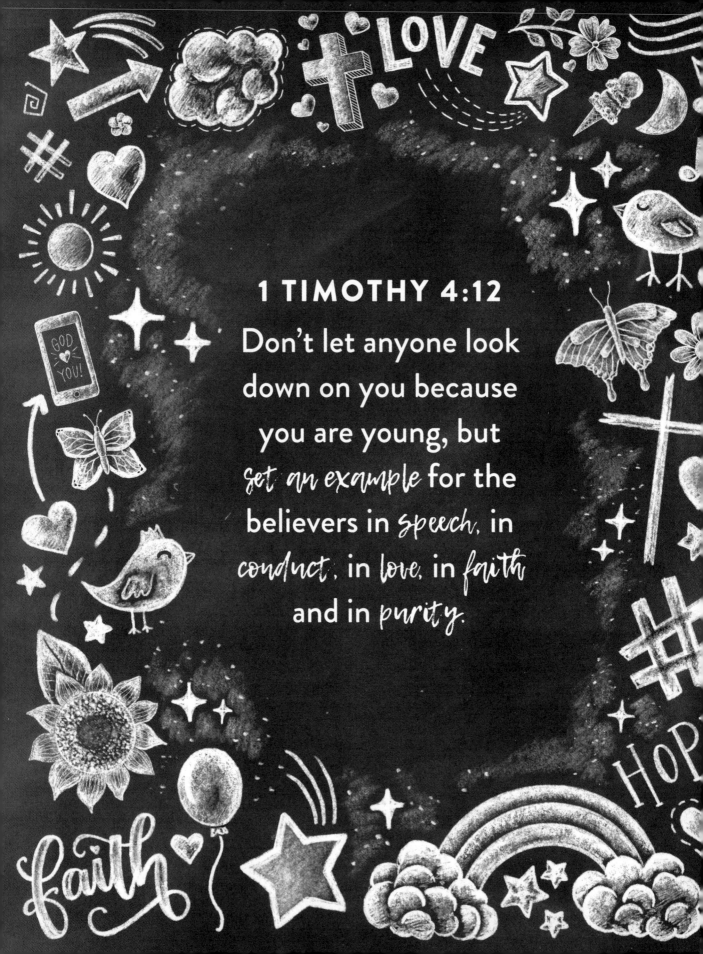

1 TIMOTHY 4:12

Don't let anyone look down on you because you are young, but *set an example* for the believers in *speech*, in *conduct*, in *love*, in *faith* and in *purity*.

REFLECT

LOVE & INNER BEAUTY

A person's age has never limited God from accomplishing His will. People like Daniel, Jeremiah, Esther, and David in the Bible were all young when God called them. Their age didn't matter to God; their hearts did. God saw past their age, insecurities, physical strength (or lack thereof), and into the core and heart of who they were and used them for His glory.

In your young age, God can also use you! Your age isn't a factor to God. He will qualify you for every road He has planned for you. Psalm 119:105 says, "Your word is a lamp for my feet, a light on my path." You're not expected to know the entire path and have it all figured out now. You need only to walk, *one step at a time*, faithfully following Him and doing your best to be a godly example to others. Keep the faith. God is with you, He loves you, and He'll never leave you!

As a believer and young person, has your age ever hindered you from accomplishing something? Has your age ever limited others from taking you seriously? How does this verse encourage you, knowing that God can use you regardless of your age or circumstances to accomplish His will for your life?

_____
_____
_____
_____
_____
_____
_____
_____
_____
_____
_____
_____
_____
_____
_____
_____
_____
_____

Reflection continued . . .

Date

LORD,
thank you

PROVERBS 15:29

The Lord is far from the wicked, but he hears the prayer of the righteous.

Things on my heart

_____
_____
_____
_____
_____
_____
_____

Highlights

_____
_____
_____
_____
_____
_____
_____
_____
_____
_____

Prayer requests

_____
_____
_____
_____
_____
_____
_____
_____
_____
_____

2 CORINTHIANS 1:3-4

Praise be to the God and Father of our Lord Jesus Christ, the Father of compassion and the God of all comfort, *who comforts us in all our troubles,* so that we can comfort those in any trouble with the comfort we ourselves receive from God.

ADVERSITY & TRIALS

When you think of the word *comfort*, what comes to mind? We feel comforted through different ways—the soft plush blanket that warms you at night, the hug from a family member or friend, or the smell that reminds you of a cherished memory. Scripture describes God as our comfort, the One who comforts us in all our troubles—not some, *all*. In turn, we can use this God-given comfort to comfort others, including our family members, friends, classmates, teammates, teachers, acquaintances, and even strangers in the checkout line at the store.

Through every struggle and trial you face in life, God is there. He knows the pain you feel and He cares (1 Peter 5:7). Each test you endure must first go through God's authority, and there is comfort knowing that in all things He works for the good of those who love Him (Romans 8:28). He can use your experiences to encourage and uplift others who will go through something similar, and He can use *you* to comfort them. For example, someone who has sustained a specific sports injury will find comfort and encouragement watching how someone else has walked through the same and come out stronger. Be encouraged that God can use the trials of your life to not only draw you closer to Him, but also give hope to others.

Do you find comfort going to God when you are faced with hardship? What people in your life comfort you when you're going through hard times? Share about a time you were able to use your experiences to comfort and encourage someone else going through something similar.

_____

_____

_____

_____

_____

_____

_____

_____

_____

_____

_____

_____

_____

_____

_____

_____

Reflection continued . . .

_____
_____
_____
_____
_____
_____
_____
_____
_____
_____
_____
_____
_____
_____
_____
_____
_____
_____
_____
_____
_____
_____
_____
_____
_____
_____
_____
_____
_____
_____
_____

Date

LORD,
thank you

_____
_____
_____
_____
_____
_____
_____
_____
_____
_____
_____
_____
_____
_____
_____
_____
_____
_____
_____
_____

PSALM 4:1

Answer me when I call to you, my righteous God. Give me relief
from my distress; have mercy on me and hear my prayer.

Things on my heart

Highlights

Prayer requests

PROVERBS 27:17

As iron sharpens iron,
so one person sharpens
another.

REFLECT

— STRENGTH THROUGH FAITH —

A blacksmith works with iron and steel. He uses a forge (think of a fiery oven) to heat these metals so they can be shaped, sharpened, and molded. Once the metal is hot, the blacksmith usually places the heated iron on an anvil and uses a tool (typically a hammer) to shape and mold the iron. The process takes time, patience, and care, but in the end, the original iron has been shaped and molded into something better than it was before. The iron is transformed as it is sharpened, hammered, and refined into something *greater*.

In the same way, God uses special instruments (typically other believers) in your life to help shape and mold you. While it is important to be a light to your non-believing friends, it is also vital to surround yourself with other Christians. Your brothers and sisters in Christ may understand the struggles you face from a different perspective than your non-Christian friends, and their insight can help and encourage you in your faith journey. Through interaction, loving discussion, and respect for one another, your minds can be sharpened, and your faith strengthened. By studying God's Word and being open to both the giving and receiving of godly wisdom, even when difficult and hard to hear, you can grow as a believer and lovingly encourage the same in others.

Do you have Christian friends or people in your life who hold you accountable and challenge you in your faith? Who are they? Have you ever challenged another Christian's actions or beliefs? If so, what happened? What areas do you desire growth in as a believer?

_____

_____

_____

_____

_____

_____

_____

_____

_____

_____

_____

_____

_____

_____

Reflection continued . . .

_____
_____
_____
_____
_____
_____
_____
_____
_____
_____
_____
_____
_____
_____
_____
_____
_____
_____
_____
_____
_____
_____
_____
_____
_____
_____
_____
_____
_____
_____
_____
_____
_____
_____

Date

LORD,
thank you

_____
_____
_____
_____
_____
_____
_____
_____
_____
_____
_____
_____
_____
_____
_____
_____
_____
_____
_____
_____
_____
_____
_____
_____

MATTHEW 18:20

"For where two or three gather in my name, there am I with them."

Things on my heart

Highlights

Prayer requests

MICAH 7:18-19

Who is a God like you, who *pardons sin and forgives the transgression* of the remnant of his inheritance? You do not stay angry forever but *delight to show mercy.* You will again have compassion on us; you will tread our sins underfoot and hurl all our iniquities into the depths of the sea.

GRACE & FORGIVENESS

The Bible is full of people who messed up, made mistakes, and needed God's grace and forgiveness for their sins. Peter, one of Jesus's twelve disciples, was one such man. He loved Jesus, followed His teachings, and was even given authority to perform miracles in Jesus's name. Even so, he denied knowing Jesus three times, just as Jesus predicted before His death on the cross. After denying Jesus the third time, Peter wept bitterly in shame and sadness (Matthew 26:69-75). However, all hope was not lost. God is a merciful, forgiving God, and Jesus reinstated Peter after His resurrection (John 21:15-19). And after Jesus ascended into heaven, Peter was filled with the Holy Spirit, and boldly preached about Jesus!

Your sins do not define you. Whatever mistakes you've made, whatever sins you've committed, bring them first and foremost to God. He knows the heart of every believer and is a loving God, full of compassion and mercy. For *all* have sinned and fall short of the glory of God (Romans 3:23)—that includes *everyone*. Yet, because of Jesus's sacrifice on the cross, the penalty for sin has been paid for! You can repent, turn to God, and seek His forgiveness. He who *makes all things new* can change your heart and restore you!

Do you ever struggle to accept God's forgiveness for the sins you've committed? If so, why? Have you accepted Jesus as your Savior, and believe that His death and resurrection on the cross serves as atonement for your sins? How does this verse encourage you, knowing that God doesn't stay angry forever, but *delights* to show mercy?

_____

_____

_____

_____

_____

_____

_____

_____

_____

_____

_____

_____

_____

_____

Reflection continued . . .

_____
_____
_____
_____
_____
_____
_____
_____
_____
_____
_____
_____
_____
_____
_____
_____
_____
_____
_____
_____
_____
_____
_____
_____
_____
_____
_____
_____
_____
_____
_____
_____
_____
_____
_____
_____

Date

LORD,
thank you

PSALM 6:9

The Lord has heard my cry for mercy; the Lord accepts my prayer.

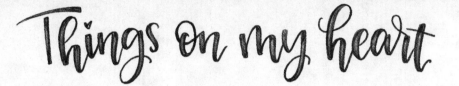

Things on my heart

Highlights

Prayer requests

PROVERBS 16:9

In their hearts humans
plan their course, but
the Lord establishes
their steps.

AWE & SOVEREIGNTY

God created you with a mind that allows you to think, plan, and solve problems. But how many times have you made plans and had them change unexpectedly? Sometimes, plans change because of situations out of your control, and sometimes they change because of your decisions, or the decisions of others. In any circumstance, it's important to remember that God is sovereign and still in control regardless of the good or bad decisions you make. He works *all* things out for the good of those who love Him (Romans 8:28), which means you can trust Him when things don't go exactly according to plan. As James says, we are to plan for things in our lives according to the Lord's will (James 4:13-15). As you trust God and submit your plans to His will, you give Him the reins to lead and guide you on the path He's planned for you—not the other way around. He loves you and knows what's best for you!

Have you ever experienced God's will prevail over the plans you initially had for yourself? What happened? What plans are you making for your life right now, and have you submitted them to God's will for you?

_____
_____
_____
_____
_____
_____
_____
_____
_____
_____
_____
_____
_____
_____
_____
_____
_____
_____
_____

Reflection continued . . .

_____
_____
_____
_____
_____
_____
_____
_____
_____
_____
_____
_____
_____
_____
_____
_____
_____
_____
_____
_____
_____
_____
_____
_____
_____
_____
_____
_____
_____
_____
_____
_____
_____
_____
_____
_____
_____
_____

Date

LORD,
thank you

_____
_____
_____
_____
_____
_____
_____
_____
_____
_____
_____
_____
_____
_____
_____
_____
_____
_____
_____
_____
_____
_____
_____
_____
_____

Whether you turn to the right or to the left, your ears will hear a
voice behind you, saying, "This is the way; walk in it."

Things on my heart

Highlights

Prayer requests

PROVERBS 19:21

Many are the plans in a person's heart, but it is the Lord's purpose that prevails.

PROVISION & FAITHFULNESS

In Scripture, the story of Daniel reminds us that God always has a plan (even when we don't understand) and rewards our faithfulness to Him (Daniel 5-6). In Daniel's story, a law was decreed that made it illegal to pray to God, the punishment being thrown in the lion's den. But in his devotion to God, Daniel continued to pray. When Daniel was caught praying to the Lord, like he did every day, King Darius gave the order for him to be thrown in the lion's den. The king, who was fond of Daniel, had been tricked into putting Daniel in the lion's den and was greatly distressed about it (Daniel 6:14).

Imagine the confusion Daniel must have felt. He had been honoring the Lord, doing what was right, and was still sentenced to the lion's den. But God rescued Daniel by sending an angel to close the mouths of the lions. The next morning, Daniel was found wound-free and King Darius was overjoyed and amazed. King Darius had the men who tricked him, and their families, thrown into the lion's den for their demise, and then issued a decree that every part of the kingdom must fear and revere God! How's that for a plot twist?

God sees beyond what you see and knows what's best for you. He's not constrained by time the way you are. Because of that, He can see the finish line before you even step up to the starting mark. He sees the bigger picture, knows what's up ahead, and you can trust Him (Psalm 9:10). When you don't understand the things happening around you, or when things don't make sense, trust that God has a plan and a purpose for everything you go through. Christians are not guaranteed a bump-free life, but God knows how to guide you through every situation. And because He is good (Psalm 34:8), you can trust and take refuge in Him.

Have you ever been verbally attacked or made fun of because of your faith? If so, what happened and how did you respond? How does this verse encourage you, knowing that God is faithful and always has a plan and purpose for the things you go through, even when they don't make sense?

_____

_____

_____

_____

_____

_____

Reflection continued . . .

LORD,
thank you

PSALM 118:5

When hard pressed, I cried to the Lord;
he brought me into a spacious place.

Things on my heart

_____
_____
_____
_____
_____
_____

Highlights

_____
_____
_____
_____
_____
_____
_____
_____
_____
_____

Prayer requests

_____
_____
_____
_____
_____
_____
_____
_____
_____

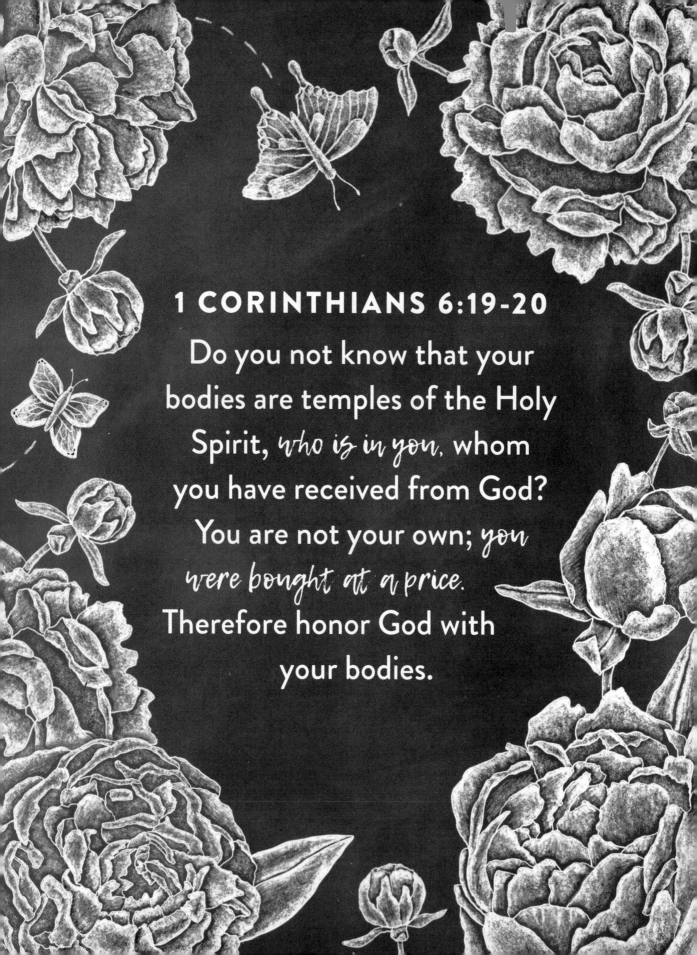

1 CORINTHIANS 6:19-20

Do you not know that your bodies are temples of the Holy Spirit, *who is in you,* whom you have received from God? You are not your own; *you were bought at a price.* Therefore honor God with your bodies.

REFLECT

GOD'S LOVE

Boundaries exist for a reason. Our homes have walls and boundaries so intruders can't enter. Our sports fields and courts have boundaries so games can be fairly played. And God gives us boundaries in Scripture so we can live a life that honors and pleases Him.

Your body is a beautiful creation given to you by God, and it's where the Holy Spirit dwells. When you became a Christian, Scripture says you were immediately filled and *sealed* with the Holy Spirit (Ephesians 1:13-14) as a guarantee of your salvation. It describes the Holy Spirit as your helper and teacher (John 14:26). This is why it's so important to honor God with your body—the Holy Spirit lives *in* you!

As a teenager, God has given you boundaries when it comes to your relationships. He's given these parameters to you out of love—not to deprive you, but *to protect you* and your heart (Proverbs 4:23)! Sex is a precious gift *created by God* that is intended to be shared between a husband and wife as the two become one (Genesis 2:24, 1 Corinthians 7:2, 1 Corinthians 7:9). 1 Corinthians 6:18 says, "Flee sexual immorality. All other sins a person commits are outside the body, but whoever sins sexually, sins against their own body." This can be especially difficult in today's society where temptations and sexually-driven messages are everywhere—on TV, the radio, the internet, and social media. The enemy uses these tactics to distort your view of sex, intimacy, and the covenant of marriage that they're meant to be shared in. This is when you can pray, read God's Word, and have fellowship with other believers to help you. You're not alone!

No matter where you find yourself today, whether this has been an area of struggle for you or not, God is faithful and forgiving. We are all (Romans 3:23) in need of God's grace, and it is only through Him that our sins and mistakes are washed away (1 John 1:9, Isaiah 43:25, Psalm 103:12, 2 Chronicles 7:14). Share your struggles, your fears, and your heart with Him. He loves you and He cares.

List some ways you can honor God with your body and in your relationships. How can you overcome the temptation to sin, and instead glorify God with the body He's given you? What does this verse mean to you?

_____

_____

_____

_____

_____

Reflection continued . . .

_____
_____
_____
_____
_____
_____
_____
_____
_____
_____
_____
_____
_____
_____
_____
_____
_____
_____
_____
_____
_____
_____
_____
_____
_____
_____
_____
_____
_____
_____
_____
_____
_____
_____
_____
_____
_____

Date

LORD,
thank you

_____
_____
_____
_____
_____
_____
_____
_____
_____
_____
_____
_____
_____
_____
_____
_____
_____
_____
_____
_____
_____

ROMANS 8:26

In the same way, the Spirit helps us in our weakness. We do
not know what we ought to pray for, but the Spirit himself
intercedes for us through wordless groans.

Things on my heart

Highlights

Prayer requests

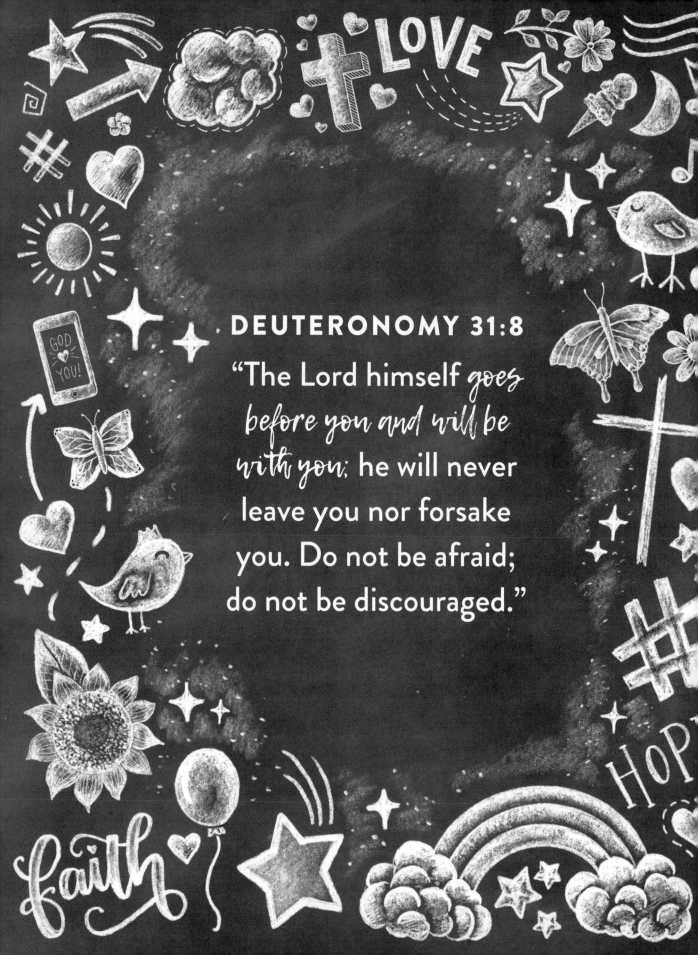

DEUTERONOMY 31:8

"The Lord himself *goes before you and will be with you*; he will never leave you nor forsake you. Do not be afraid; do not be discouraged."

FER

In the gospels, Jesus displayed His splendor and authority over nature when He walked on water and calmed the wind at sea (Matthew 14:22-33, John 6:16-21, Mark 6:45-52). Immediately following the feeding of the five thousand, Jesus sent His disciples in a boat to cross over a lake. The wind and the waves were strong and overwhelmed their boat. But Jesus went to the disciples, walking on the water toward them! Notice how Jesus went *toward* them while they were in the midst of the storm? He didn't abandon them, but rather moved closer to them as they struggled. In the book of Matthew, Jesus invited Peter, one of His disciples, to walk out to Him on the water. As Peter got out of the boat and walked on the water toward Jesus, Peter noticed the wind and was immediately filled with fear. He began to sink and cried out for Jesus to save him. In response, Jesus reached out his hand and caught Peter, asking why he had so little faith. Then, Jesus climbed into the boat with Peter, and the wind died down.

As a Christian and follower of Jesus, there will be ups and downs. Because of sin, the world is imperfect. However, we have hope because of our faith in Jesus and His unconditional love for us! When the storm you're facing seems too big and you're afraid, Jesus is there to embrace you and give you peace. Notice how it was when Peter took his eyes *off* Jesus that He began to feel afraid and sink. This is a reminder for you to keep our eyes on Him, especially in the midst of the storm. Whether the storms you face involve school, your friends or family, an injury or illness, or things outside of your control, no fear, hardship, or trouble you endure is too great for Him, because He has overcome the world (John 16:33)!

How does your faith in God sustain you through life's ups and downs? Share about a time God rescued you from a storm you faced. How does this verse encourage you?

_____

_____

_____

_____

_____

_____

_____

_____

_____

_____

_____

Reflection continued . . .

_____
_____
_____
_____
_____
_____
_____
_____
_____
_____
_____
_____
_____
_____
_____
_____
_____
_____
_____
_____
_____
_____
_____
_____
_____
_____
_____
_____
_____
_____
_____
_____
_____
_____
_____
_____
_____
_____
_____
_____

Date

LORD
thank you

JONAH 2:2

He said: "In my distress I called to the Lord, and he answered me.
From deep in the realm of the dead I called for help,
and you listened to my cry."

Things on my heart

Highlights

Prayer requests

PSALM 119:9

How can a young
person stay on the path
of purity? By living
according to your word.

LOVE & INNER BEAUTY

Have you ever thrown out an instruction manual, thinking you have things figured out, only to realize how vital those instructions truly are? You finally understand that those instructions were given to you in order to *help* you, not hinder you. The Bible is like God's instruction manual for our lives and tells the beautiful story of Jesus. It is God-breathed (2 Timothy 3:16), alive and active, and sharper than a double-edged sword (Hebrews 4:12). It is no mistake or coincidence that it has survived thousands of years and continues to transform lives all over the world.

As a young lady, you are a beautiful, God-created soul, and your purity matters to God. Purity encompasses not only sexuality (1 Thessalonians 4:3-8, 1 Corinthians 6:18), but so much more, including your actions (Galatians 5:19-21, Luke 6:31), your words (Ephesians 4:29), and your thoughts (Philippians 4:8). The TV shows, websites, and music you expose yourself to, the way you act in your relationships and on social media, the people you surround yourself with, the words you speak, and your clothing are all areas of your life you can take captive in order to protect yourself and your purity. God's Word teaches us to avoid the things of the world (1 John 2:15-17) and the works of the flesh. Instead, we are to set our minds on things above (Colossians 3:2)—on the things that please and honor God. God's Word is full of encouragement and truth, and it has the answers to your toughest questions about how to live a life that brings glory to Him. The world paints a false picture of what "normal" conduct and behavior looks like, but by having the truth of God's Word in your heart, you can combat those false notions, resist temptation, and stay on the path of purity.

What does a pure life look like to you? What areas of your life can you take captive in order to protect your purity? How can you resist your earthly nature to sin and instead live a pure life that pleases God?

_____

_____

_____

_____

_____

_____

_____

_____

_____

_____

Reflection continued . . .

_____

_____

_____

_____

_____

_____

_____

_____

_____

_____

_____

_____

_____

_____

_____

_____

_____

_____

_____

_____

_____

_____

_____

_____

_____

_____

_____

_____

_____

_____

_____

_____

_____

_____

_____

_____

_____

Date

LORD,
thank you

PHILIPPIANS 1:9-11

And this is my prayer: that your love may abound more and more in knowledge and depth of insight, so that you may be able to discern what is best and may be pure and blameless for the day of Christ, filled with the fruit of righteousness that comes through Jesus Christ—to the glory and praise of God.

Things on my heart

Highlights

Prayer requests

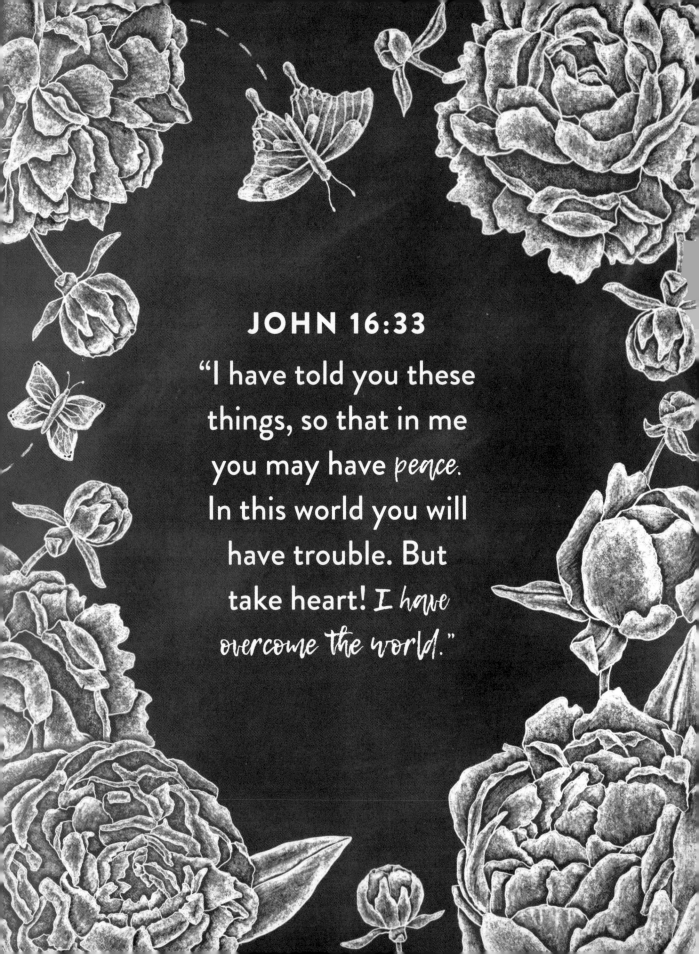

JOHN 16:33

"I have told you these
things, so that in me
you may have *peace*.
In this world you will
have trouble. But
take heart! *I have
overcome the world.*"

ADVERSITY & TRIALS

Going through hard times is just that—hard. Because we live in a broken world, there are good days, bad days, and some in between. In Scripture, Jesus told the disciples that they would have trouble, as in, it was inevitable (John 16:33). There was no, "maybe there will be trouble," but rather "you *will* have trouble." Those words still stand true today. Being a Christian doesn't exclude you from going through trials and hardship, because you are human just like everyone else, living in an imperfect world.

In Scripture, Paul and James counted it as joy to suffer for Christ (Romans 5:3-5, James 1:2-4). Most of us don't look at suffering with joy, so how were they able to rejoice *while* suffering? Paul and James knew trials serve a bigger purpose as they produce perseverance, character, and hope. Trials draw us closer to God, change our perspective, and give us empathy for others. And those are things to rejoice about. Paul was content in whatever situation he found himself in, good or bad, because He had faith in God and trusted His plan (Philippians 4:10-13). John 14:27 says, "Peace I leave with you; my peace I give you. I do not give to you as the world gives. Do not let your hearts be troubled and do not be afraid." God is with you, and He loves you!

Have you ever been able to find joy and/or peace in the midst of a trial? If so, what happened? How can you view trials going forward from a godly perspective the way that Paul and James did? What does this verse mean to you?

_____

_____

_____

_____

_____

_____

_____

_____

_____

_____

_____

_____

_____

_____

_____

Reflection continued . . .

_____
_____
_____
_____
_____
_____
_____
_____
_____
_____
_____
_____
_____
_____
_____
_____
_____
_____
_____
_____
_____
_____
_____
_____
_____
_____
_____
_____
_____
_____
_____
_____
_____
_____

Date

LORD,
thank you

_____
_____
_____
_____
_____
_____
_____
_____
_____
_____
_____
_____
_____
_____
_____
_____
_____
_____
_____
_____
_____

PSALM 143:1

Lord, hear my prayer, listen to my cry for mercy; in your
faithfulness and righteousness come to my relief.

Things on my heart

_____
_____
_____
_____
_____
_____

Highlights

_____
_____
_____
_____
_____
_____
_____
_____
_____
_____
_____

Prayer requests

_____
_____
_____
_____
_____
_____
_____
_____
_____
_____
_____

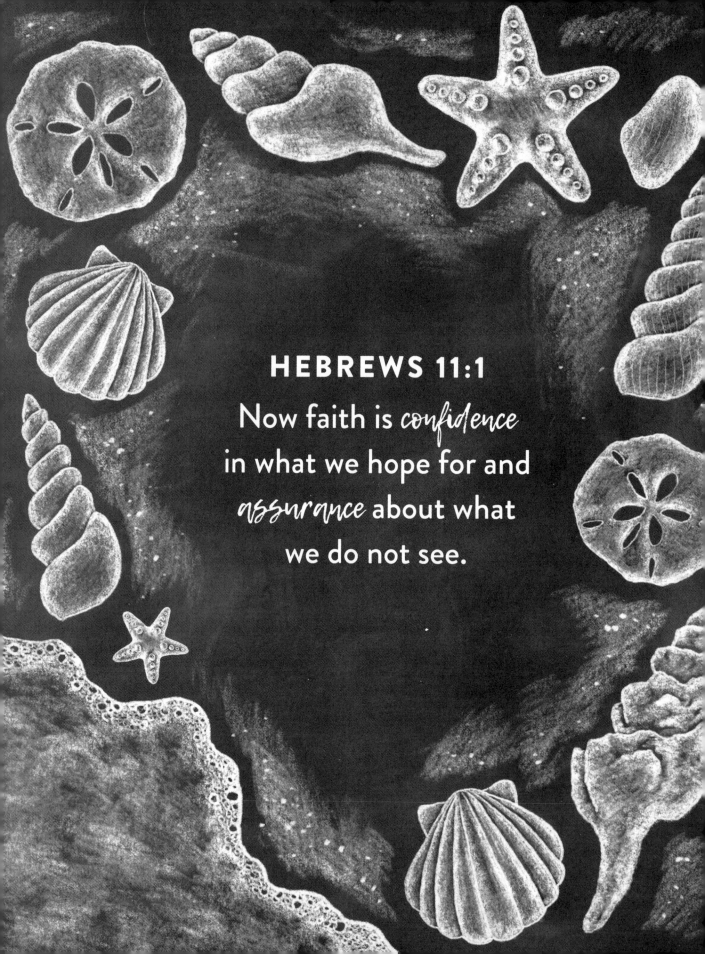

HEBREWS 11:1

Now faith is *confidence*
in what we hope for and
assurance about what
we do not see.

REFLECT

STRENGTH THROUGH FAITH

The story of Noah paints a beautiful illustration of what it means to walk in faith. Noah was a righteous man of God during a time when the world was full of sin and corruption. God instructed Noah to build an ark (a huge boat) that would save him, his family, and the creatures of the earth from a flood that would destroy every other living land being (Genesis 7-9:17, Genesis 7:21-23). Noah was divinely warned by God about things *he could not yet see*, and what did he do? He moved with godly fear and faith and built the ark as God instructed (Hebrews 11:7). His act of faith saved him, his household, and the creatures of the earth from destruction. Notice that Noah acted by building the ark, *then God moved* by calling the creatures to the ark and flooding the earth. Noah's act of faith *preceded* God's glorious act to save him, his family, and the animals! That's what faith is! Just like Noah, we can live a God-glorifying and honoring life as we love others, walk by faith, and trust in God's love and sovereignty.

As Christians, we are called to walk by faith, not by sight (2 Corinthians 5:7). While we cannot physically see God, His evidence is all around. Look at the mountains, the trees, the ocean, the incredible creatures of the Earth, and *you*! God's creation alone gives us confirmation that He exists (Romans 1:20)! And while we don't have physical arks to build like Noah did, we have obstacles and challenges we are called to walk through in faith and a beautiful destination waiting for us in heaven with Him!

Do you ever wrestle with your faith in God or His existence when difficult things happen? Why or why not? Share about a time you walked in faith through something and watched God move with you.

_____

_____

_____

_____

_____

_____

_____

_____

_____

_____

_____

_____

Reflection continued . . .

_____
_____
_____
_____
_____
_____
_____
_____
_____
_____
_____
_____
_____
_____
_____
_____
_____
_____
_____
_____
_____
_____
_____
_____
_____
_____
_____
_____
_____
_____
_____
_____
_____
_____
_____

Date

LORD,
thank you

_____
_____
_____
_____
_____
_____
_____
_____
_____
_____
_____
_____
_____
_____
_____
_____
_____
_____
_____
_____
_____

PSALM 17:6

I call on you, my God, for you will answer me;
turn your ear to me and hear my prayer.

Things on my heart

_____
_____
_____
_____
_____
_____

Highlight

_____
_____
_____
_____
_____
_____
_____
_____
_____
_____

Prayer requests

_____
_____
_____
_____
_____
_____
_____
_____
_____
_____

1 JOHN 1:9

If we *confess* our sins,
he is faithful and just
and will *forgive* us our
sins and *purify* us from
all unrighteousness.

GRACE & FORGIVENESS

King David is known for many amazing things in the Old Testament. With God's help, David slayed the giant Goliath, was appointed to become the second king of Israel, and led his people into many victorious battles. He is also credited for writing many of the Psalms and loved God (Psalm 18:1). He is described as "a man after God's own heart" more than once in Scripture (1 Samuel 13:14, Acts 13:22) and God loved him.

But David was not without sin. He broke many of the Ten Commandments (Exodus 20:1-17, Deuteronomy 5:3-22), including murder and adultery, but God *still* forgave him! Rather than running away from God in his guilt and shame, David turned *toward* God, confessing his sins and asking for forgiveness (Psalm 51), and God forgave him (2 Samuel 12:13). While there were still consequences for David's sin, God continued to love and work through him. And through David's lineage, our perfect sinless Savior and King, Jesus Christ, came into the world (Jeremiah 23:5-6).

God forgives all sins. He sees your heart and knows when you are truly repentant for the sins you've committed. While there are consequences for your sins, as we see in the life of King David, God can still use you for His perfect purpose. You are never too far from Him to turn, repent, and change your ways. He can restore and transform you from the inside out (Psalm 23:3)!

Share about a time you experienced God's grace, forgiveness, and restoration after falling victim to sin. How did this experience change you? How does this verse encourage you?

_____
_____
_____
_____
_____
_____
_____
_____
_____
_____
_____

Reflection continued . . .

_____
_____
_____
_____
_____
_____
_____
_____
_____
_____
_____
_____
_____
_____
_____
_____
_____
_____
_____
_____
_____
_____
_____
_____
_____
_____
_____
_____
_____
_____
_____
_____
_____
_____
_____
_____
_____
_____
_____

Date

LORD,
thank you

_____
_____
_____
_____
_____
_____
_____
_____
_____
_____
_____
_____
_____
_____
_____
_____
_____
_____
_____
_____
_____
_____

You, Lord, are forgiving and good, abounding in
love to all who call to you.

Things on my heart

_____
_____
_____
_____
_____
_____
_____

Highlights

_____
_____
_____
_____
_____
_____
_____
_____
_____
_____
_____

Prayer requests

_____
_____
_____
_____
_____
_____
_____
_____
_____
_____
_____

PSALM 37:4

Take delight in the Lord,
and he will give you the
desires of your heart.

REFLECT

AWE & SOVEREIGNTY

Desires, goals, hopes, dreams, wants. We all have these in some shape or form, but what does it mean to "delight yourself in the Lord and He will give you *the desires of your heart*?" Does it mean that if you delight in the Lord, you'll get that new cell phone you've been wanting, or your dream car? Does it mean you'll grow three inches taller, get straight A's next quarter, or get your dream job and life right after graduation? Not quite.

The phrase "to delight in" means to find joy, pleasure, and/or satisfaction in something. When your joy and satisfaction are rooted in the Lord, your desires *change*. They become more aligned with His desires. Things that are important to God become important to you. Your peace and fulfillment become less focused on your circumstances—what you have and don't have—and more grounded in God's truth and promises. If God is for you, who can be against you (Romans 8:31)? Talk to Him and share what's on your heart.

Oftentimes, the goals and desires we have coincide with our God-given talents and abilities. This is how God uses you and your abilities to impact the world right where you are! Your passion for art may be God leading you into the design world. A talent and passion for singing may be God leading you into ministry through song. Are you a talented athlete? Maybe God is leading you into the sports world to shine a light to other athletes around you. Share the desires you have with Him and trust Him to do with them what He knows is best for you!

What are some of your heart's greatest desires? Do you find it easy to share these desires with God? Why or why not? What hopes and desires has God already fulfilled in your life?

_____

_____

_____

_____

_____

_____

_____

_____

_____

_____

_____

_____

_____

Reflection continued . . .

Date

LORD,
thank you

The Lord is near to all who call on him, to all who call on him in truth. He fulfills the desires of those who fear him; he hears their cry and saves them.

Things on my heart

Highlights

Prayer requests

133

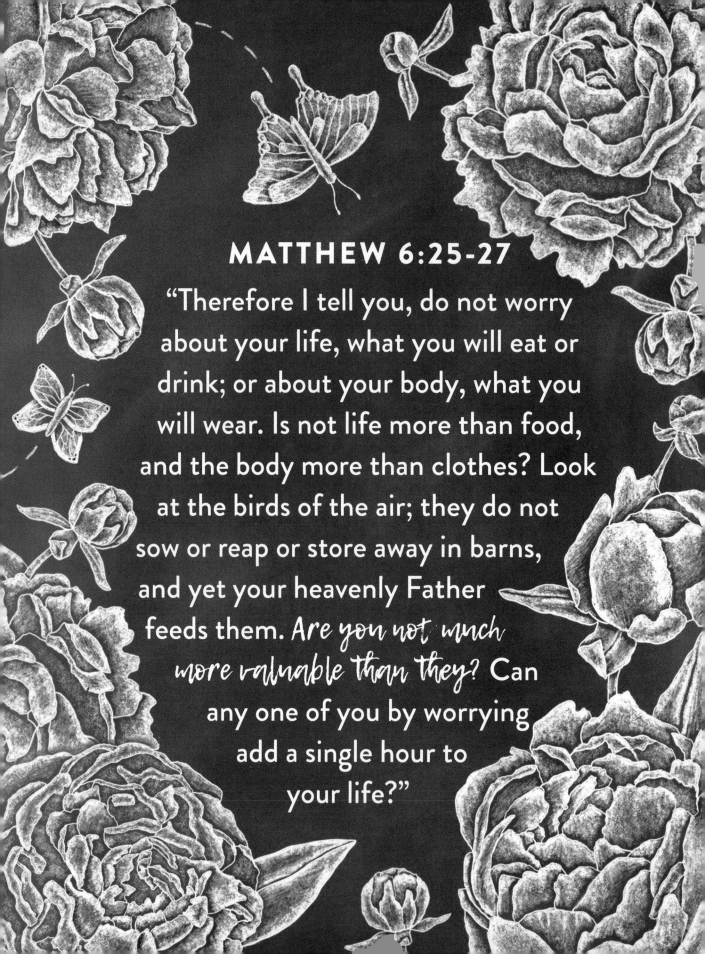

MATTHEW 6:25-27

"Therefore I tell you, do not worry about your life, what you will eat or drink; or about your body, what you will wear. Is not life more than food, and the body more than clothes? Look at the birds of the air; they do not sow or reap or store away in barns, and yet your heavenly Father feeds them. *Are you not much more valuable than they?* Can any one of you by worrying add a single hour to your life?"

Reflect

PROVISION & FAITHFULNESS

When Moses led the Israelites out of Egypt into the wilderness, their basic needs like food and water became very apparent. However, God knew what they needed and provided for them. He sent manna from heaven (Exodus 16), which was like bread. He sent quail for meat and gave them water to drink. Any food the Israelites stored up "just in case" became rotten and spoiled overnight. This taught them that they could fully rely on God, His promises, and His faithfulness through the daily ups and downs they endured in the desert. But oh, how often they forgot this!

In the same way, God knows what you need. He values you much more than the birds and yet He still provides for them daily! Rather than worrying about your day-to-day struggles, which won't change the outcome, you can pray to your Heavenly Father who loves you and knows what you need before you even ask (Psalm 139:4)!

What types of things worry you, and which of those things are out of your control? How can you approach each day with confidence knowing that God values you (even more than the birds that He provides for daily)?

Reflection continued . . .

_____
_____
_____
_____
_____
_____
_____
_____
_____
_____
_____
_____
_____
_____
_____
_____
_____
_____
_____
_____
_____
_____
_____
_____
_____
_____
_____
_____
_____
_____
_____
_____
_____
_____

Date

LORD
thank you

_____
_____
_____
_____
_____
_____
_____
_____
_____
_____
_____
_____
_____
_____
_____
_____
_____
_____
_____
_____
_____
_____
_____
_____
_____

And when you pray, do not keep on babbling like pagans, for they think they will be heard because of their many words. Do not be like them, for your Father knows what you need before you ask him.

Things on my heart

Highlights

Prayer requests

JAMES 1:16-17

Don't be deceived, my dear brothers and sisters. Every good and perfect gift is from above, coming down from the Father of the heavenly lights, who does not change like shifting shadows.

REFLECT

GOD'S LOVE

Presents are fun, aren't they? They make you feel cared for, loved, and the anticipation of opening them is so exciting! That joyful feeling you get when you receive a gift speaks volumes about who God is. Scripture says that *every* good and perfect gift is from above, and that includes you (you were gifted to your parents)!

The gifts you've received and the blessings you have are all from God. He is the author of good! God is light and there is no darkness in Him at all (1 John 1:5). God offers us the biggest gift of all—our salvation—through the death and resurrection of His Son, Jesus Christ. All the other good things in life are a bonus, and He lovingly gives them to us, because that's who He is. God is love (1 John 4:8, 1 John 4:16) and He doesn't change. Shadows move, shift, and change shape depending on the position of the sun, but God is constant, He is good, and He loves you!

What gifts has God blessed your life with? Have you thanked Him? How does this verse change your perspective on giving and receiving gifts?

_____

_____

_____

_____

_____

_____

_____

_____

_____

_____

_____

_____

_____

_____

_____

_____

_____

_____

_____

_____

Reflection continued . . .

_____

_____

_____

_____

_____

_____

_____

_____

_____

_____

_____

_____

_____

_____

_____

_____

_____

_____

_____

_____

_____

_____

_____

_____

_____

_____

_____

_____

_____

_____

_____

_____

_____

Date

LORD
thank you

If you, then, though you are evil, know how to give good gifts to
your children, how much more will your Father in heaven give
good gifts to those who ask him!

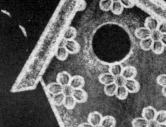

Things on my heart

_____

_____

_____

_____

_____

_____

_____

Highlights

_____

_____

_____

_____

_____

_____

_____

_____

_____

Prayer requests

_____

_____

_____

_____

_____

_____

_____

_____

1 PETER 5:6-7

Humble yourselves, therefore, under God's mighty hand, that he may lift you up in due time. Cast all your anxiety on him because *he cares for you.*

FEAR

When you hear someone bragging about themselves in an "I'm better than you" manner, what's your first thought? For many, this type of behavior creates tension and pushes people away. It's called pride and is a trait God opposes (James 4:6, 1 Peter 5:5, Proverbs 3:34). A humble person creates the opposite feeling. Someone who is humble knows their abilities and gifts, but doesn't flaunt them arrogantly to the world. In today's society, this can be tough, especially with pressures from all sides (and the ever-growing social media) to act and look a certain way. Social media often sends the notion that your value depends on your best selfie (don't forget that filter!), your best dance moves, and how many followers or likes you have. God sees beyond all of that!

God values the beauty of a gentle and quiet spirit (1 Peter 3:4). When you humble yourself before God, you're acknowledging that He is the supreme authority—that you are in fact a tiny speck in an enormous universe, created and unconditionally loved *by Him*! Tell Him about your anxieties and the pressures you feel, and let Him lift you up in His perfect timing (James 4:10).

Do you feel societal pressure to behave or act a certain way? Do any of these pressures make you anxious? How can you focus on staying humble before the Lord when the world sends the opposite message?

_____

_____

_____

_____

_____

_____

_____

_____

_____

_____

_____

_____

_____

_____

_____

_____

_____

Reflection continued . . .

_____
_____
_____
_____
_____
_____
_____
_____
_____
_____
_____
_____
_____
_____
_____
_____
_____
_____
_____
_____
_____
_____
_____
_____
_____
_____
_____
_____
_____
_____
_____
_____
_____
_____
_____
_____
_____
_____
_____
_____
_____

Date

LORD,
thank you

_____
_____
_____
_____
_____
_____
_____
_____
_____
_____
_____
_____
_____
_____
_____
_____
_____
_____
_____
_____
_____

JEREMIAH 29:12

Then you will call on me and come and pray to me,
and I will listen to you.

Things on my heart

Highlights

Prayer requests

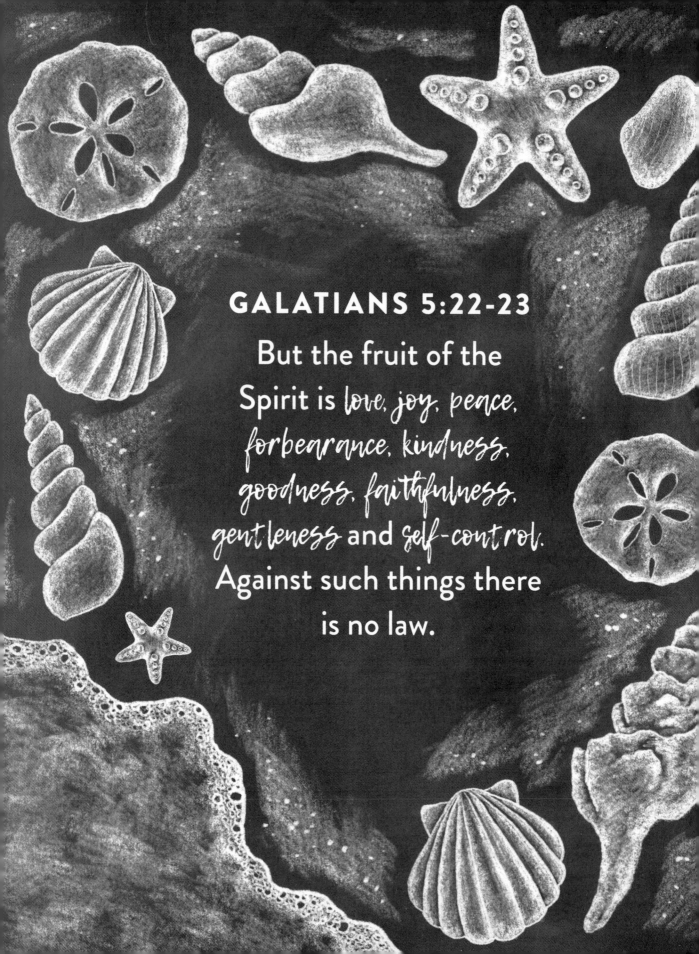

GALATIANS 5:22-23

But the fruit of the Spirit is love, joy, peace, forbearance, kindness, goodness, faithfulness, gentleness and self-control. Against such things there is no law.

REFLECT

LOVE & INNER BEAUTY

When you became a Christian, you became a new creation (2 Corinthians 5:17), filled with the Holy Spirit! You are no longer condemned by a sinful nature, but sealed with the Holy Spirit as a guarantee of your forgiveness and salvation! In Scripture, Paul describes the conflict between the Christian's flesh and spirit (Galatians 5:17). Though you are saved, you are still an imperfect human being. Your flesh (your body) is still prone to worldly desires and sin, but now your spirit is filled with the Holy Spirit and His fruit—love, joy, peace, forbearance (or patience), kindness, goodness, faithfulness, gentleness, and self-control.

Notice in this verse how Paul uses the term "fruit" to describe all nine, rather than multiple "fruits." With the indwelling of the Holy Spirit, *all nine* are present; not one in some Christians, three in another Christian, all nine! While our behaviors and actions may not always reflect them due to our sinful natures, we can access and demonstrate all nine because of the Holy Spirit living within us! And over time, we can mature and grow this fruit! In the same way that fruit starts as a seed, your faith and spiritual growth can take time. But by studying God's Word, following it, surrounding yourself with other believers, and honoring God, your spiritual fruit can grow, mature, and outpour to those around you. The Holy Spirit helps you and guides you in truth (John 16:13-15). You are called to live by the Spirit and let His indwelling transform you from the inside out.

Which specific fruit(s) do you desire growth in, and which one(s) comes more naturally for you? What can you do to grow and mature in the fruit of the Spirit? Share about a time you were able to access the fruit of the Spirit through a challenging situation.

Reflection continued . . .

_____
_____
_____
_____
_____
_____
_____
_____
_____
_____
_____
_____
_____
_____
_____
_____
_____
_____
_____
_____
_____
_____
_____
_____
_____
_____
_____
_____
_____
_____
_____
_____
_____
_____
_____
_____

Date

LORD,
thank you

LUKE 3:21-11

When all the people were being baptized, Jesus was baptized too. And as he was praying, heaven was opened and the Holy Spirit descended on him in bodily form like a dove. And a voice came from heaven: "You are my Son, whom I love; with you I am well pleased."

Things on my heart

_____
_____
_____
_____
_____
_____

Highlights

_____
_____
_____
_____
_____
_____
_____
_____
_____
_____

Prayer requests

_____
_____
_____
_____
_____
_____
_____
_____
_____
_____

1 CORINTHIANS 15:33-34

Do not be misled: "Bad company corrupts good character." Come back to your senses as you ought, and *stop sinning;* for there are some who are ignorant of God—I say this to your shame.

ADVERSITY & TRIALS

The people we surround ourselves with and the friends we choose impact us. While there is both good and bad peer pressure, bad peer pressure is when your peers (the people your age or grade) put pressure on you to do things you know in your heart to be wrong before God. This type of pressure puts you in a predicament. You can either go along and give in to the pressure, or you can stand firm and choose not to participate. Not giving in and choosing to do what honors God can sometimes create an awkward dichotomy of feeling left out. But that's the point. As a Christian, you *already* stand out! Through Christ, you have been set apart and are called to be different, to go against the norms of the world.

Your true friends will love you for who you are. They will build you up, encourage you, hold you accountable, and help you grow in your faith—not pull you away from it. They won't pressure you to act in ways you know to be wrong. As Scripture says, "He who walks with the wise grows wise, but a companion of fools suffers harm" (Proverbs 13:20).

Which friends can you count on to help you do what's right, and which friends rely on you? Share about a time when you were able to stand firm in the face of peer pressure and do the right thing. How did you feel overcoming it?

_____
_____
_____
_____
_____
_____
_____
_____
_____
_____
_____
_____
_____
_____
_____
_____

Reflection continued . . .

_____
_____
_____
_____
_____
_____
_____
_____
_____
_____
_____
_____
_____
_____
_____
_____
_____
_____
_____
_____
_____
_____
_____
_____
_____
_____
_____
_____
_____
_____
_____
_____
_____
_____

Date

LORD,
thank you

JAMES 5:13

Is anyone among you in trouble? Let them pray. Is anyone happy?
Let them sing songs of praise.

Things on my heart

Highlights

Prayer requests

PHILIPPIANS 4:13

I can do *all* this through
him who gives me
strength.

STRENGTH THROUGH FAITH

When you think of strength, what comes to mind? Lifting weights? Emotional strength? Spiritual strength? In context, Paul used these words when he was in prison for preaching about the gospel of Jesus Christ. In the words leading up to this verse, he talks about how he has learned to be content *whatever the circumstances*: "I know what it is to be in need, and I know what it is to have plenty. I have learned the secret of being content in any and every situation, whether well fed or hungry, whether living in plenty or in want. *I can do all this through him who gives me strength*" (Philippians 4:12-13).

Notice how Paul's description of strength has more to do with enduring the ebbs and flows and ups and downs of life. Paul's attitude wasn't dependent on his circumstances, but rather on his hope in Jesus. Regardless of your circumstances, you have a Savior who loves you and is your source of joy and strength (Psalm 16:11, Nehemiah 8:10). We will all experience mountains and valleys in life, but by being rooted in our faith, we can find strength to endure anything life throws our way!

Has God ever allowed a trial or difficult time in your life that served to strengthen your faith in Him? If so, what happened? How does this verse encourage you going forward through the mountains and valleys of life knowing that you can do all things through Christ who strengthens you?

_____

_____

_____

_____

_____

_____

_____

_____

_____

_____

_____

_____

_____

_____

Reflection continued . . .

_____
_____
_____
_____
_____
_____
_____
_____
_____
_____
_____
_____
_____
_____
_____
_____
_____
_____
_____
_____
_____
_____
_____
_____
_____
_____
_____
_____
_____
_____
_____
_____
_____
_____
_____
_____
_____
_____
_____
_____

Date

LORD thank you

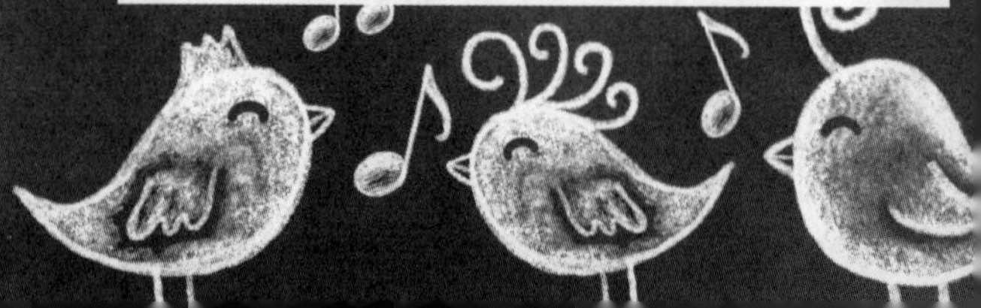

_____
_____
_____
_____
_____
_____
_____
_____
_____
_____
_____
_____
_____
_____
_____
_____
_____
_____
_____
_____

ACTS 2:21

And everyone who calls on the name of the Lord will be saved.

Things on my heart

_____

_____

_____

_____

_____

_____

Highlights

_____

_____

_____

_____

_____

_____

_____

_____

_____

Prayer requests

_____

_____

_____

_____

_____

_____

_____

_____

_____

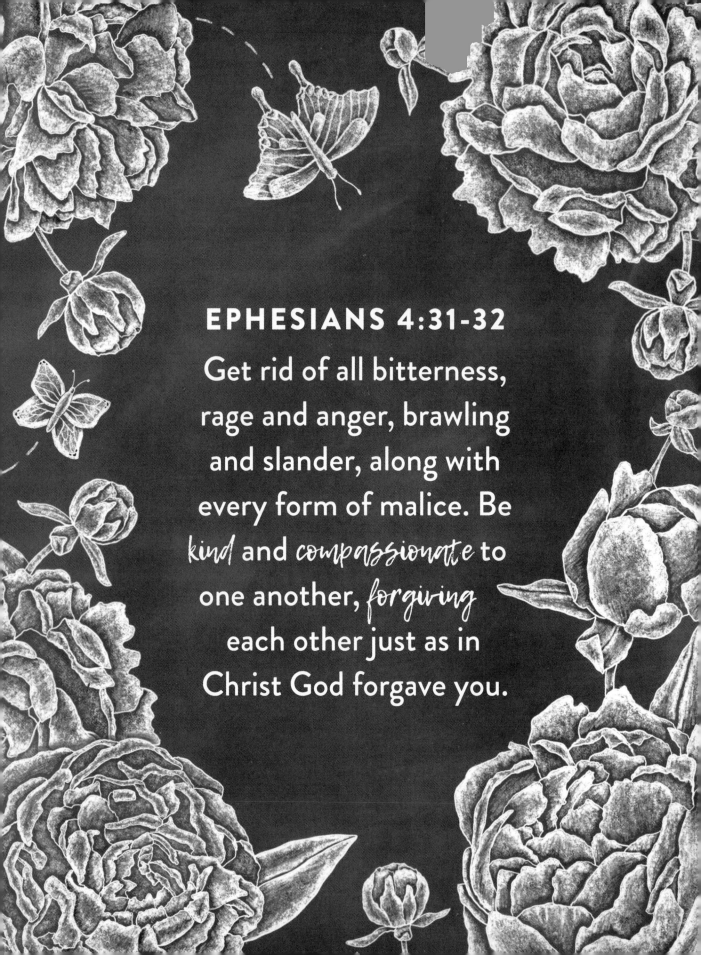

EPHESIANS 4:31-32

Get rid of all bitterness, rage and anger, brawling and slander, along with every form of malice. Be *kind* and *compassionate* to one another, *forgiving* each other just as in Christ God forgave you.

GRACE & FORGIVENESS

Forgiveness can be difficult. When you feel wronged, mistreated, and misunderstood, what's typically your first reaction? Are you the type to lash out, or the type to say nothing while letting your frustration grow within you? While being angry itself is not a sin, Scripture warns about not sinning *while* you're angry (Ephesians 4:26). It's what you do while angry that determines if you're in the wrong or not. Scripture talks about not repaying evil for evil, but to overcome evil with good, leaving any wrath up to God (Romans 12:17-21)—which is often easier said than done!

It's important to remember that *nobody* is perfect, and no one is without sin. "For *all* have sinned and fall short of the glory of God" (Romans 3:23). We all make mistakes. It is only by the grace of God that we are justified and forgiven of our sins through Jesus Christ. In turn, we are to follow Jesus's example, extending grace and forgiveness to those who have wronged us (Matthew 18:21-22, Mark 11:25).

How do you feel when someone forgives you? Does forgiveness come easily for you? Why or why not? How can you follow Jesus's example and live a life filled with grace and forgiveness toward others, even when it's difficult?

_____
_____
_____
_____
_____
_____
_____
_____
_____
_____
_____
_____
_____
_____
_____
_____

Reflection continued . . .

_____
_____
_____
_____
_____
_____
_____
_____
_____
_____
_____
_____
_____
_____
_____
_____
_____
_____
_____
_____
_____
_____
_____
_____
_____
_____
_____
_____
_____
_____
_____
_____
_____
_____
_____
_____
_____

Date

LORD,
thank you

_____
_____
_____
_____
_____
_____
_____
_____
_____
_____
_____
_____
_____
_____
_____
_____
_____
_____
_____

MARK 11:24-25

"Therefore I tell you, whatever you ask for in prayer, believe that you have received it, and it will be yours. And when you stand praying, if you hold anything against anyone, forgive them, so that your Father in heaven may forgive you your sins."

Things on my heart

_____
_____
_____
_____
_____
_____

Highlights

_____
_____
_____
_____
_____
_____
_____
_____
_____
_____
_____

Prayer requests

_____
_____
_____
_____
_____
_____
_____
_____
_____
_____

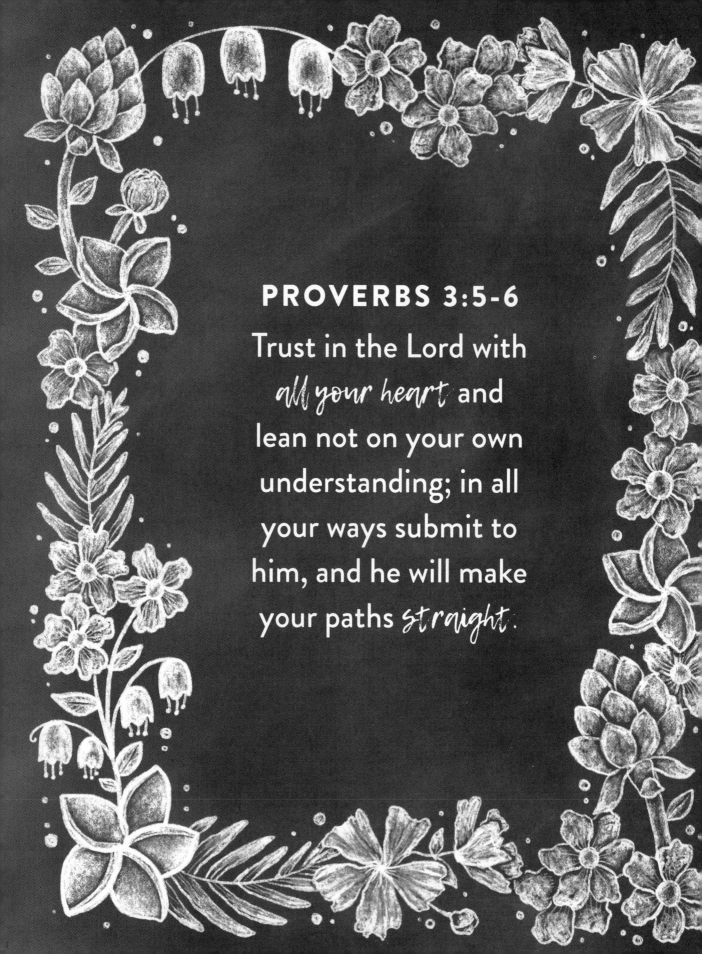

PROVERBS 3:5-6

Trust in the Lord with *all your heart* and lean not on your own understanding; in all your ways submit to him, and he will make your paths *straight*.

AWE & SOVEREIGNTY

When going on a hike, it's repeatedly advised to "stay on the path." By staying on the path, your chance of staying safe from uneven footing and wildlife that calls the wilderness its home increases. But what happens if your path suddenly has a "detour" sign that takes you down a route you're not familiar with? What do you do? Do you follow, trusting that whoever placed the sign there knows something you don't? Or do you turn and go back the way you came out of fear of the unknown?

Life can be similar to hiking in the wilderness. There will be twists and turns and unfamiliar detours along the way, and at times they might be scary and confusing. When you put your faith and trust in the Lord, remembering that He loves you and knows what's best for you, then you can confidently follow the path (and plans) He has for you, even when you feel unsure. Scripture says, "For my thoughts are not your thoughts, neither are your ways my ways," declares the Lord. "As the heavens are higher than the earth, so are my ways higher than your ways and my thoughts than your thoughts" (Isaiah 55:8-9). He sees beyond your present circumstances, beyond the detours and bumps in the road, and He knows how to get you where He desires you to be. Keep the faith!

Has God ever allowed something in your life that made you question His goodness or love for you? If so, what happened? How might this verse encourage you through the ups and downs and detours of life going forward?

_____

_____

_____

_____

_____

_____

_____

_____

_____

_____

_____

_____

_____

Reflection continued . . .

_____
_____
_____
_____
_____
_____
_____
_____
_____
_____
_____
_____
_____
_____
_____
_____
_____
_____
_____
_____
_____
_____
_____
_____
_____
_____
_____
_____
_____
_____
_____
_____
_____
_____
_____
_____
_____
_____
_____

Date

LORD,
thank you

Devote yourselves to prayer, being watchful and thankful.

Things on my heart

Highlights

Prayer requests

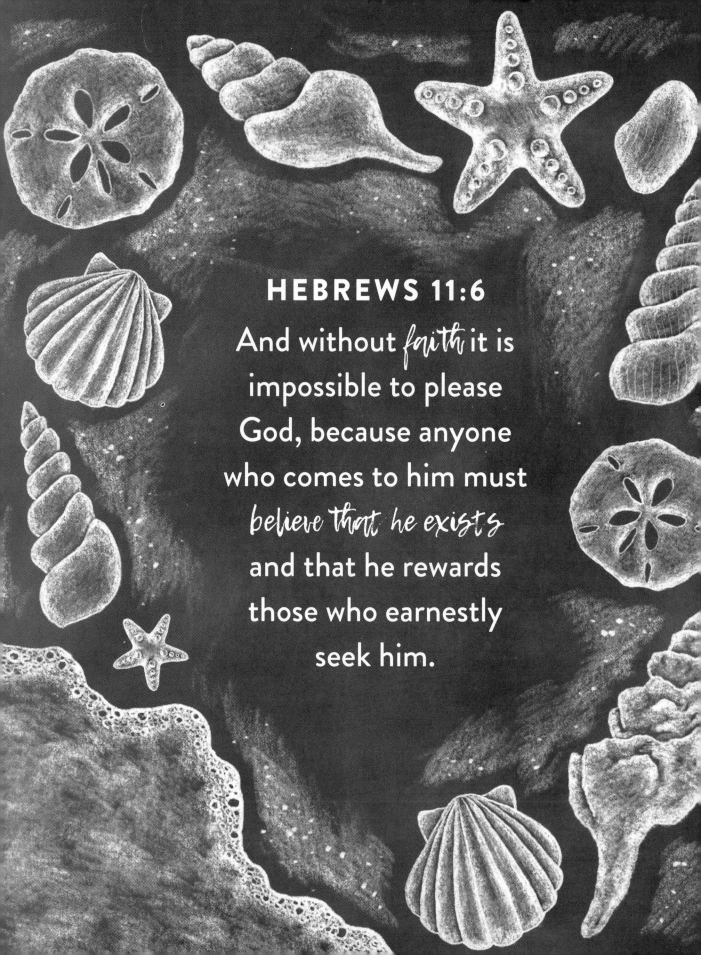

HEBREWS 11:6
And without *faith* it is
impossible to please
God, because anyone
who comes to him must
believe that he exists
and that he rewards
those who earnestly
seek him.

PROVISION & FAITHFULNESS

Joshua, the appointed leader of the Israelites after the death of Moses, was called by God to lead the Israelites into the Promised Land. Along the way, there were numerous obstacles, yet Joshua remained faithful to God, trusted His provision and walked in courageous faith, obedient to God.

After crossing the Jordan River by foot, God gave specific directions regarding the city of Jericho (Joshua 5:13-6:27). For six days, the armed Israelites (along with the ark of the covenant and seven priests sounding trumpets) were instructed to march around the city of Jericho once per day. They were not to make a sound with their voices during this time. On the seventh day, they marched around the city seven times as the priests blew the trumpets. It was on this seventh time that Joshua commanded the people to shout, and *only then* did the walls of Jericho fall! Joshua and the Israelites acted in faith by obeying God's specific instructions, and God knocked down the walls of Jericho! God rewarded their faithfulness to Him and provided the city of Jericho as He had promised.

It can be hard to walk in faith when there seems to be countless obstacles or "Jerichos" in front of you. Perhaps you're working through some tough classes, or you're dealing with the reality of an injury or illness, or maybe you're dealing with family drama. Whatever you're going through, God sees you right where you are and He knows the challenges you face. He walks these "battles" with you so you're not alone. Walking in faith requires you to trust and act in obedience to Him and His calling for you, even when the obstacles in front of you seem impossible. If God can knock down the walls of an entire city after acts of faith, imagine what He can do for you!

What "Jerichos" in your life has God knocked down for you? Are you currently facing any "Jerichos?" If so, what are they? Share about a time you witnessed or experienced God's faithfulness.

_____
_____
_____
_____
_____
_____
_____

Reflection continued . . .

_____
_____
_____
_____
_____
_____
_____
_____
_____
_____
_____
_____
_____
_____
_____
_____
_____
_____
_____
_____
_____
_____
_____
_____
_____
_____
_____
_____
_____
_____
_____
_____
_____
_____
_____

Date

LORD
thank you

_____
_____
_____
_____
_____
_____
_____
_____
_____
_____
_____
_____
_____
_____
_____
_____
_____
_____
_____
_____
_____
_____
_____

MATTHEW 6:6

But when you pray, go into your room, close the door and pray to your Father, who is unseen. Then your Father, who sees what is done in secret, will reward you.

Things on my heart

Highlights

Prayer requests

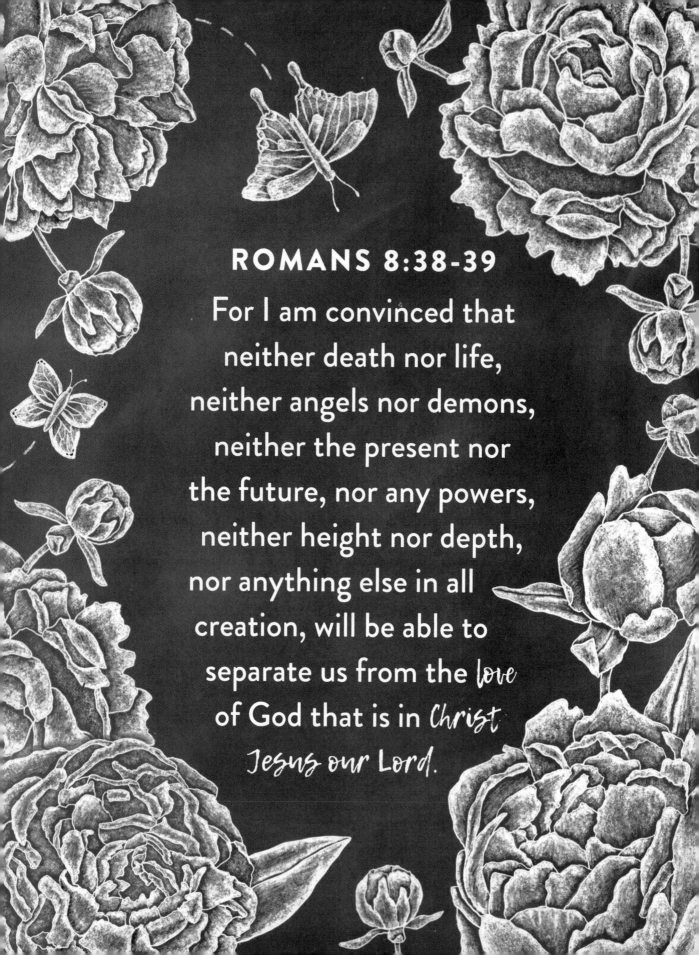

ROMANS 8:38-39

For I am convinced that
neither death nor life,
neither angels nor demons,
neither the present nor
the future, nor any powers,
neither height nor depth,
nor anything else in all
creation, will be able to
separate us from the *love*
of God that is in *Christ
Jesus our Lord.*

GOD'S LOVE

Sometimes we feel our choices have pushed us far from God. We fear that He no longer loves us, or that our difficult circumstances are a result of Him no longer loving us. But this is not true. *Nothing* can separate you from the love of God. Nothing!

Because of sin and the fallen, imperfect world we live in, our punishment as a human race was death and eternal separation from God. However, God loved you so much that He sent His only Son, Jesus Christ, to die on the cross as an atonement for your sins so that you could have a relationship with Him. Now, through your faith and acceptance of Jesus Christ, you're reconciled to God (Romans 5:10)! That's how much He loves you!

Have you ever felt that God didn't love you, or that you were undeserving of His love? If so, why? Have your circumstances ever made you doubt His love for you? How does this verse encourage you, knowing that nothing can separate you from God's love that is in Christ Jesus?

_____

_____

_____

_____

_____

_____

_____

_____

_____

_____

_____

_____

_____

_____

_____

_____

_____

_____

Reflection continued . . .

_____
_____
_____
_____
_____
_____
_____
_____
_____
_____
_____
_____
_____
_____
_____
_____
_____
_____
_____
_____
_____
_____
_____
_____
_____
_____
_____
_____
_____
_____
_____
_____
_____
_____
_____
_____
_____
_____

Date

LORD,
thank you

PSALM 66:20

Praise be to God, who has not rejected my prayer or
withheld his love from me!

Things on my heart

_____

_____

_____

_____

_____

_____

Highlights

_____

_____

_____

_____

_____

_____

_____

_____

_____

_____

Prayer requests

_____

_____

_____

_____

_____

_____

_____

_____

_____

_____

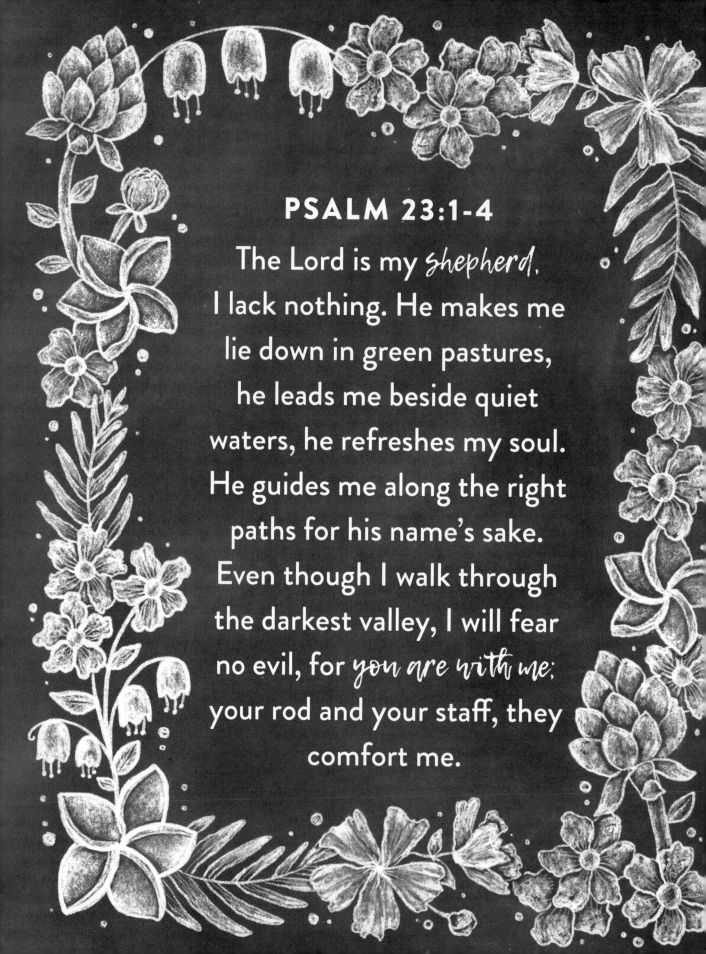

PSALM 23:1-4

The Lord is my *shepherd*,
I lack nothing. He makes me
lie down in green pastures,
he leads me beside quiet
waters, he refreshes my soul.
He guides me along the right
paths for his name's sake.
Even though I walk through
the darkest valley, I will fear
no evil, for *you are with me;*
your rod and your staff, they
comfort me.

FEER

When traditional farming practices were more prevalent (especially in ancient times), a shepherd was used to watch over a flock of sheep. The shepherd's responsibility was to look over, protect, and tend to the flock. When danger lurked nearby, the shepherd would use his rod (imagine a long, wooden, club-like stick) to strike and fend off predators in order to protect the sheep from harm. When a sheep would wander in the wrong direction or become entangled in brush or rocks, the shepherd would use his staff (imagine a long walking stick with a rounded hook on the end, like a candy cane shape), to redirect it back to safety.

In Scripture, Jesus refers to himself as the Good Shepherd (John 10:11, John 10:14) and us as His sheep. In the same way that a shepherd loves, leads, and protects his flock, Jesus loves, guides, and protects us! When we wander or are entangled in opposition, difficulty, or fear, we're not alone. Jesus, our shepherd, walks *with us* to guide, protect, and redirect us as needed. The shepherd loves his sheep, and Jesus loves you so much that He was willing to lay down his life to save you! While you might feel afraid of the unknown, the difficulties, and the dangers and pressures of the world, you can rest in God's comfort and guidance. He is with you and loves you! He has overcome the world (John 16:33), and if God is for you, who can be against you (Romans 8:31)?

Have you ever gotten lost or wandered in the wrong direction? If so, what happened? How can you approach each day with confidence rather than fear, knowing that God, your Shepherd, loves you, watches over you, and walks with you every step of the way?

_____

_____

_____

_____

_____

_____

_____

_____

_____

_____

_____

_____

_____

Reflection continued . . .

_____
_____
_____
_____
_____
_____
_____
_____
_____
_____
_____
_____
_____
_____
_____
_____
_____
_____
_____
_____
_____
_____
_____
_____
_____
_____
_____
_____
_____
_____
_____
_____
_____
_____

Date

LORD,
thank you

_____
_____
_____
_____
_____
_____
_____
_____
_____
_____
_____
_____
_____
_____
_____
_____
_____
_____
_____
_____

My sheep listen to my voice; I know them, and they follow me.
I give them eternal life, and they shall never perish; no one will
snatch them out of my hand.

Things on my heart

Highlights

Prayer requests

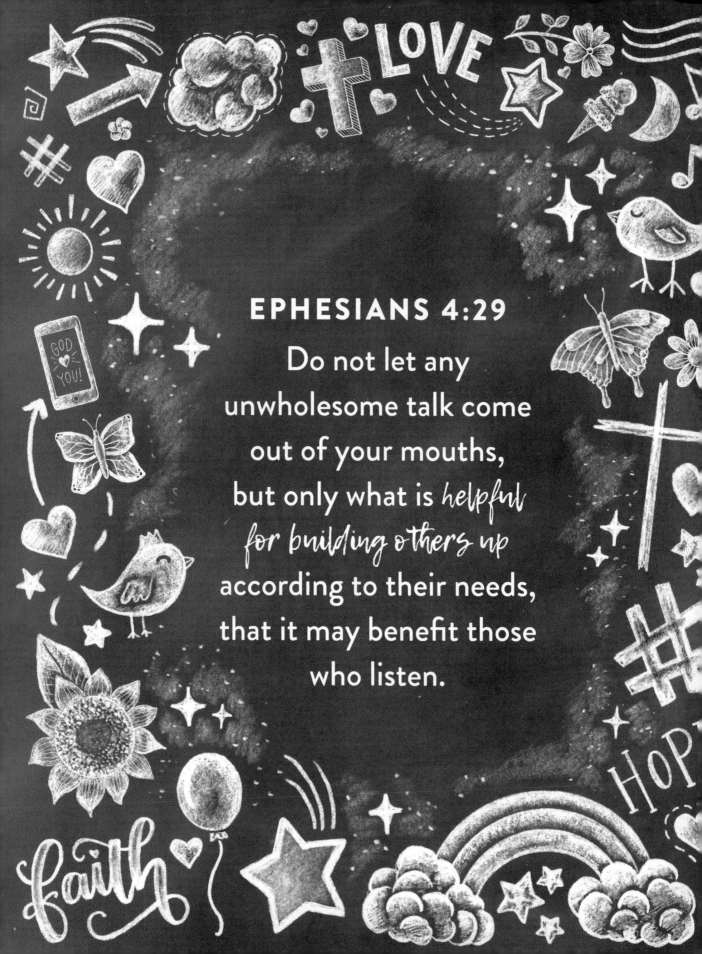

EPHESIANS 4:29

Do not let any unwholesome talk come out of your mouths, but only what is *helpful for building others up* according to their needs, that it may benefit those who listen.

LOVE & INNER BEAUTY

The human tongue may be small, but it packs a powerful punch. In Scripture, the human tongue is compared to a spark of fire and is called a world of evil among the parts of our bodies (James 3:5-6). In the same way that a spark of fire can lead to a raging forest fire, misuse of the tongue can cause pain and destruction to those around us. Ironically, we use our tongue to both praise God *and* hurt others (James 3:9-10), and this should not be. This is why it's so important to use wisdom and to think before speaking, especially when emotions are involved and/or we feel wronged. We will all be held accountable to Christ for the empty words we speak (Matthew 12:36). Scripture says no human can tame the tongue. But by reading God's Word, seeking His wisdom, and living by the Spirit, we can do our best to overcome the detrimental power of the tongue.

In what ways do you struggle with taming your tongue? Is it difficult for you to speak kindly when you feel wronged? How can you conquer your tongue when you feel angry or upset and use it for good instead?

Reflection continued . . .

_____
_____
_____
_____
_____
_____
_____
_____
_____
_____
_____
_____
_____
_____
_____
_____
_____
_____
_____
_____
_____
_____
_____
_____
_____
_____
_____
_____
_____
_____
_____
_____
_____
_____
_____
_____

Date

LORD,
thank you

_____
_____
_____
_____
_____
_____
_____
_____
_____
_____
_____
_____
_____
_____
_____
_____
_____
_____
_____
_____
_____
_____

But to you who are listening I say. Love your enemies, do good
to those who hate you, bless those who curse you, pray for
those who mistreat you."

Things on my heart

_____

_____

_____

_____

_____

Highlights

_____

_____

_____

_____

_____

_____

_____

_____

_____

_____

Prayer requests

_____

_____

_____

_____

_____

_____

_____

_____

_____

_____

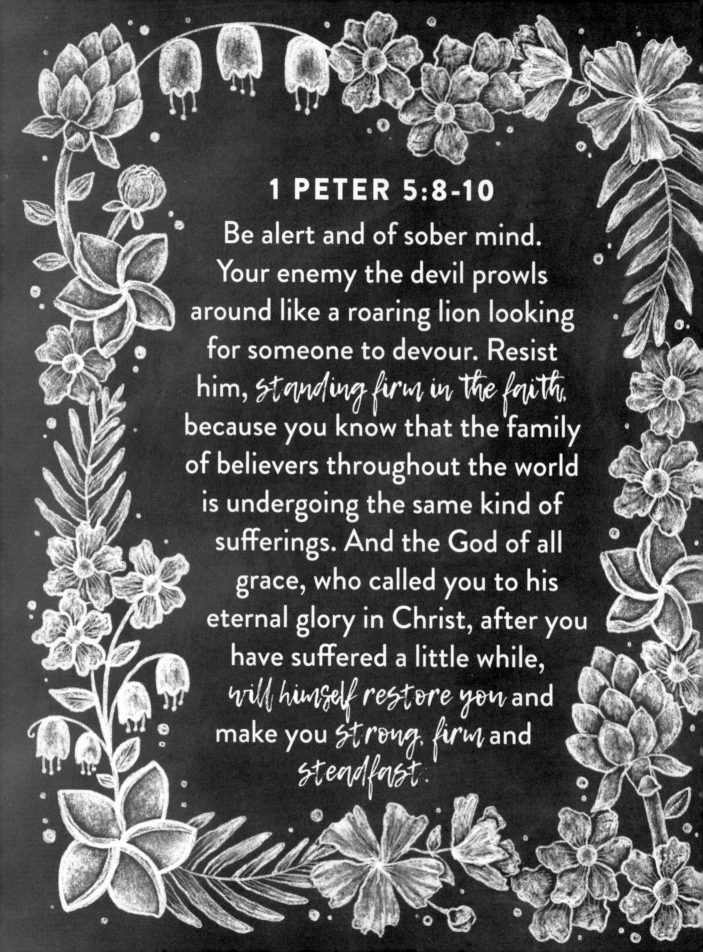

1 PETER 5:8-10

Be alert and of sober mind. Your enemy the devil prowls around like a roaring lion looking for someone to devour. Resist him, *standing firm in the faith,* because you know that the family of believers throughout the world is undergoing the same kind of sufferings. And the God of all grace, who called you to his eternal glory in Christ, after you have suffered a little while, *will himself restore you* and make you *strong, firm* and *steadfast.*

ADVERSITY & TRIALS

As Christians, we are never promised a bump-free life. In fact, Jesus himself said that we *would* have trouble in this world, but that we could take heart, because he has *overcome* the world (John 16:33)! Sometimes it's hard to keep the faith when we are enduring hardship. Why would a loving God allow pain, heartache, and suffering? Why would a loving God allow temptations and trials to come to His loved ones? These are questions the enemy uses to distract and destroy our relationship with God, but this is where we can put on the full armor of God to help us stand firm in our faith (Ephesians 6:10-17). It's important to remember that God tempts no one (James 1:13), but that through Him, we can overcome! James 4:7 says to "Submit your-selves, then, to God. Resist the devil and he will flee from you." God has a plan and a purpose for your life, even through the tough stuff. When you don't understand what's happening to you or around you, or you're caught in an area of temptation, go to God. Pray to Him, read His Word, journal your thoughts to Him, and listen for His voice. Surround yourself with other believers who can support and encourage you. You are not meant to fight your battles alone! Submit to God, trust Him, and let Him fight your battles for you (Exodus 14:14). He is your rock and your salvation (Psalm 62:2).

When you are enduring trials, temptation, and suffering, how do you find strength? Who are the people in your life you count on to encourage and uplift you when you're going through tough times? Share about a time when you encountered God's strength through a tempting situation and overcame it.

_____

_____

_____

_____

_____

_____

_____

_____

_____

_____

_____

_____

_____

_____

_____

Reflection continued . . .

_____
_____
_____
_____
_____
_____
_____
_____
_____
_____
_____
_____
_____
_____
_____
_____
_____
_____
_____
_____
_____
_____
_____
_____
_____
_____
_____
_____
_____
_____
_____
_____
_____
_____
_____
_____
_____
_____

Date

LORD,
thank you

Now this I know: The Lord gives victory to his anointed. He answers him from his heavenly sanctuary with the victorious power of his right hand.

Things on my heart

Highlights

Prayer requests

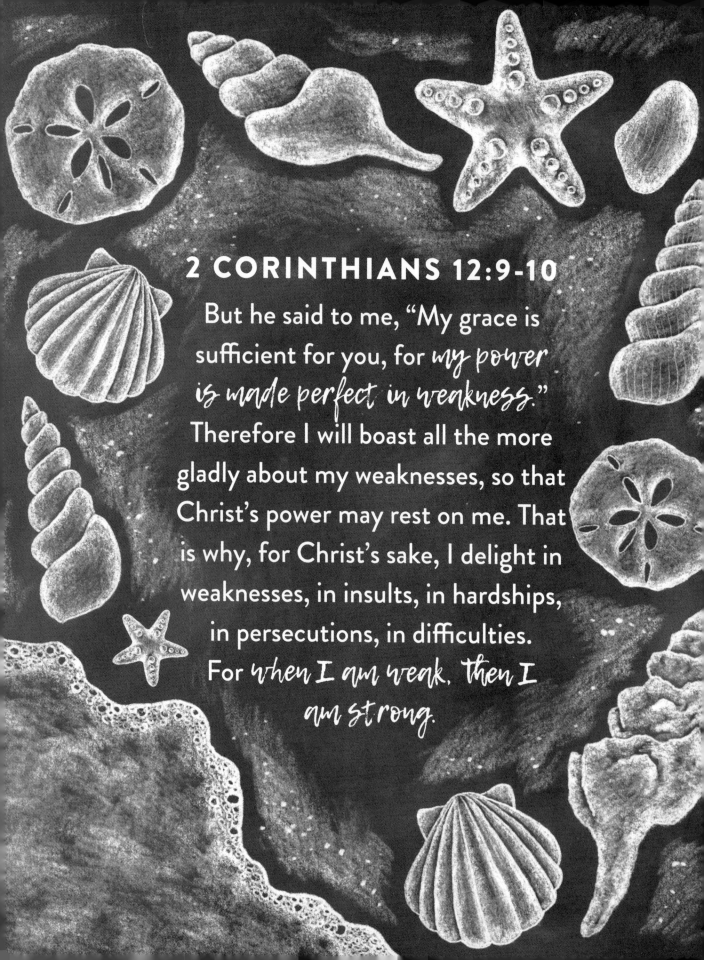

2 CORINTHIANS 12:9-10

But he said to me, "My grace is sufficient for you, for *my power is made perfect in weakness.*" Therefore I will boast all the more gladly about my weaknesses, so that Christ's power may rest on me. That is why, for Christ's sake, I delight in weaknesses, in insults, in hardships, in persecutions, in difficulties. For *when I am weak, then I am strong.*

REFLECT

STRENGTH THROUGH FAITH

Paul endured numerous trials and suffering after becoming saved. During his missions in spreading the message of Jesus Christ, he was imprisoned, flogged, whipped, beaten, exposed to death numerous times, chained, plotted against, shipwrecked, stoned, bitten by a snake, and many other trials (2 Corinthians 11:23-26, Acts 16:23, Acts 21:33, Acts 23:2, Acts 23:12, Acts 27, Acts 28:3).

Paul also had what Scripture refers to as "a thorn in his flesh." While we aren't sure exactly what this was, we know it was something difficult that God allowed (2 Corinthians 12:7-8). And by the power of Jesus Christ, Paul remained faithful, was able to endure, stand firm, and find strength to keep going! It was in Paul's times of weakness that the power of Jesus was revealed. He performed extraordinary miracles like raising a man from the dead, surviving a viper snake bite, healing the sick, and more, all because of Jesus's power resting on him in spite of the trials he was enduring (Acts 19:11-12, Acts 20:9-12, Acts 28:3-6, Acts 28:7-10)!

It's when we're weak that God is our strength (Isaiah 40:29). When you feel overwhelmed by what's happening around you or to you, by the assignments you need to complete, by an injury or diagnosis, by the endless to-do lists, and the pressures you feel, lean into Jesus! He will give you the rest you need (Matthew 11:28-30) and fight your battles for you (Exodus 14:14)!

Share about a time that Christ's power rested on you through a weakness of yours. What happened? How did you feel?

_____
_____
_____
_____
_____
_____
_____
_____
_____
_____
_____
_____

Reflection continued . . .

_____
_____
_____
_____
_____
_____
_____
_____
_____
_____
_____
_____
_____
_____
_____
_____
_____
_____
_____
_____
_____
_____
_____
_____
_____
_____
_____
_____
_____
_____
_____
_____
_____
_____
_____

Date

LORD, thank you

_____
_____
_____
_____
_____
_____
_____
_____
_____
_____
_____
_____
_____
_____
_____
_____
_____
_____
_____
_____
_____

But I tell you, love your enemies and pray for those who persecute you, that you may be children of your Father in heaven. He causes his sun to rise on the evil and the good, and sends rain on the righteous and the unrighteous.

Things on my heart

Highlights

Prayer requests

ROMANS 12:1-2

Therefore, I urge you, brothers and sisters, in view of God's mercy, to offer your bodies as a *living sacrifice*, holy and pleasing to God—this is your true and proper worship. Do not conform to the pattern of this world, but *be transformed* by the renewing of your mind. Then you will be able to test and approve what God's will is—*his good, pleasing and perfect will.*

GRACE & FORGIVENESS

When you became saved and accepted Jesus as your savior, you were immediately filled with the Holy Spirit and became *a new creation* (2 Corinthians 5:17). For many, this can be a confusing concept, because you still have the same body and you're still you. However, the Holy Spirit's indwelling sets you apart from the nonbeliever and is what makes you a child of God (John 1:12, 1 John 3:1, Romans 8:16). You are no longer condemned for your sins, because Jesus bore them all when He died on the cross—and your acceptance of Him as your savior sets you free from the consequences of them (Romans 8:2). The renewing of your mind comes from the Holy Spirit's work within you (Titus 3:5-6), and is ongoing. As you read God's Word and seek Him, your faith grows and your mind becomes more in tune with Him.

Offering your body as a living sacrifice means you no longer live for yourself—you live for God. By not conforming to the world, you choose to put God's desires for you first and foremost, to honor Him, and to live according to His Word. Sometimes this is easier said than done. It's easy to get caught up in things of the world—temptations, social media and who has the most followers, the newest tech gadget or fashion trend, fitting in with the kids at school, being the best at your extracurricular activity, and the list goes on. But with God, you're not alone in your fight to honor Him and do what's right. "For you were once darkness, but now you are light in the Lord. Live as children of light" (Ephesians 5:8). Seek God, read His Word, have fellowship with other believers, and trust His good, pleasing, and perfect will.

In what ways do you struggle with conforming to the world? How can you be intentional about putting God's desires and will for you above worldly desires? What does this verse mean to you?

Reflection continued . . .

_____
_____
_____
_____
_____
_____
_____
_____
_____
_____
_____
_____
_____
_____
_____
_____
_____
_____
_____
_____
_____
_____
_____
_____
_____
_____
_____
_____
_____
_____
_____
_____
_____
_____

Date

LORD,
thank you

The end of all things is near. Therefore be alert and
of sober mind so that you may pray.

Things on my heart

Highlights

Prayer requests

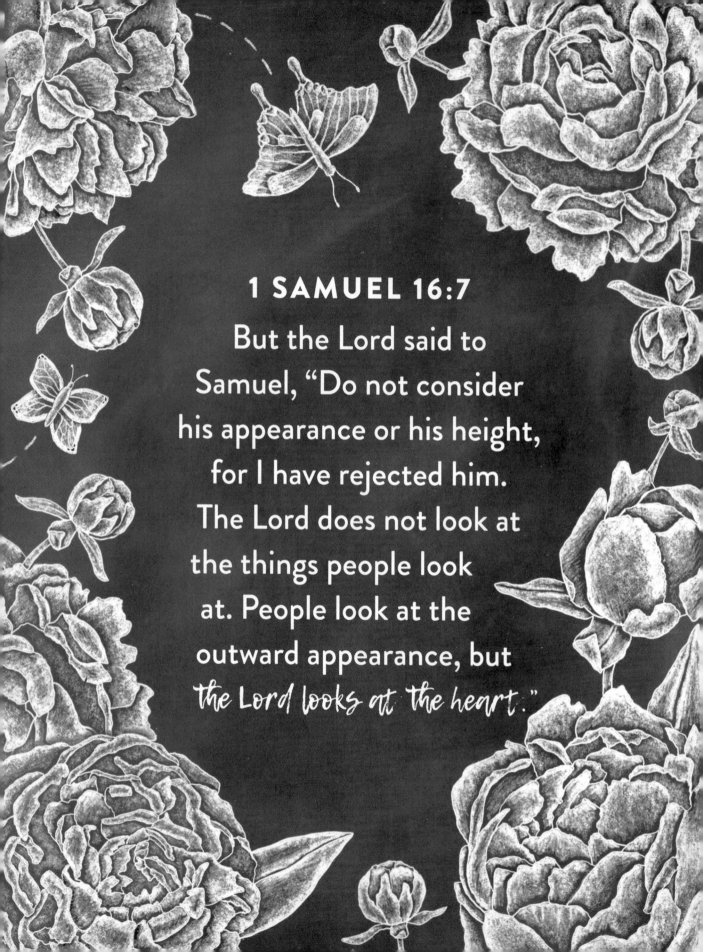

1 SAMUEL 16:7

But the Lord said to Samuel, "Do not consider his appearance or his height, for I have rejected him. The Lord does not look at the things people look at. People look at the outward appearance, but *the Lord looks at the heart.*"

AWE & SOVEREIGNTY

The phrase "Don't judge a book by its cover" is a popular metaphor used to show that you shouldn't judge something's worth by looking at the outward appearance alone. In Scripture, this happened when Samuel, a prophet of the Lord, was sent to Bethlehem to anoint David as the new king of Israel. Before Samuel knew that David was God's chosen king, Samuel noticed his brother, Eliab. Based on Eliab's physical appearance alone, Samuel thought that surely he was the Lord's anointed (1 Samuel 16:6). But instead, God had chosen Eliab's shepherd brother David, the youngest of his family.

The concept of judging someone by their appearance has been around a long time. Through your peers, social media, magazines, and the internet, the world says that you have to look and dress a certain way in order to be considered beautiful or worthy of recognition. But God sees past your height, weight, the makeup you wear or don't wear, the way you style your hair, and your style of clothes. He doesn't care how many social media followers you have or how popular you are in school. What matters to God is *your heart*. That's where your beauty comes from—*from within*. He is intimately acquainted with you, so much so that He knows the number of hairs on your head (Matthew 10:30) and you are fearfully and wonderfully made by Him (Psalm 139:14)!

Have you ever judged someone by their appearance? How did your assumptions about them change when you got to know them on a personal level? How can you remember to focus each day on what God sees as beautiful rather than what the world pushes?

Reflection continued . . .

_____
_____
_____
_____
_____
_____
_____
_____
_____
_____
_____
_____
_____
_____
_____
_____
_____
_____
_____
_____
_____
_____
_____
_____
_____
_____
_____
_____
_____
_____
_____
_____
_____
_____
_____
_____
_____
_____

Date

LORD,
thank you

JEREMIAH 33:3

'Call to me and I will answer you and tell you great and
unsearchable things you do not know.'

Things on my heart

_____
_____
_____
_____
_____
_____

Highlights

_____
_____
_____
_____
_____
_____
_____
_____
_____

Prayer requests

_____
_____
_____
_____
_____
_____
_____
_____
_____

LAMENTATIONS 3:22-23

Because of the Lord's great love we are not consumed, for *his compassions never fail.* They are new every morning; *great is your faithfulness.*

PROVISION & FAITHFULNESS

Have you ever watched a sunrise in the morning? The moment the sun breaks the plane of your vision is the moment God's glorious light show begins! As the sun rises higher in the sky, the light and everything it touches becomes more beautiful and vibrant. The colors become richer and the shadows of night fade away. Every sunrise is an opportunity for a new beginning, and a fresh start.

Each morning is symbolic in that the light *breaks through* the darkness! In the same way, because of God's faithfulness and through your relationship with Christ, you can overcome any darkness (sin, hardship, trials) in your life (2 Thessalonians 3:3). God's love, mercies, and compassions for you never stop. They are new *every* morning! Because of this, you can confidently approach God with the mistakes you've made, the trials you've endured, and the thoughts occupying your mind. His love never ends, and He wants to hear from you, His adored creation! As Hebrews 4:16 says, "Let us then approach God's throne of grace with confidence, so that we may receive mercy and find grace to help us in our time of need."

Do you struggle with forgiving yourself for things in your past? Why or why not? How can you live in freedom and approach God confidently, knowing that He loves you and His mercies for you are new every morning?

Reflection continued . . .

_____
_____
_____
_____
_____
_____
_____
_____
_____
_____
_____
_____
_____
_____
_____
_____
_____
_____
_____
_____
_____
_____
_____
_____
_____
_____
_____
_____
_____
_____
_____

Date

LORD
thank you

_____
_____
_____
_____
_____
_____
_____
_____
_____
_____
_____
_____
_____
_____
_____
_____
_____
_____
_____
_____
_____
_____
_____
_____
_____
_____
_____
_____

In the morning, Lord, you hear my voice; in the morning I lay my
requests before you and wait expectantly.

Things on my heart

Highlights

Prayer requests

LUKE 15:3-7

Then Jesus told them this parable: "Suppose one of you has a hundred sheep and loses one of them. Doesn't he leave the ninety-nine in the open country and *go after the lost sheep* until he finds it? And when he finds it, he joyfully puts it on his shoulders and goes home. Then he calls his friends and neighbors together and says, 'Rejoice with me; I have found my lost sheep.' I tell you that in the same way there will be more rejoicing in heaven over one sinner who repents than over ninety-nine righteous persons who do not need to repent."

REFLECT

GOD'S LOVE

In Scripture, Jesus often spoke in parables to teach His followers. Parables were like short stories that had underlying spiritual and moral lessons. In the parable of the lost sheep, we learn that because of His great love for us, *God pursues us*, even when we've wandered like sheep on the wrong path! Jesus, your Good Shepherd (John 10:11), laid down His life on the cross for you, *because He loves you*. "For God so loved the world that he gave his one and only Son, that whoever believes in him shall not perish but have eternal life" (John 3:16).

Whether you are currently in tune with God or wandering on your own, God's love for you is infinite! As we learn from this parable, there is rejoicing in heaven when you repent and follow Him. He is an unconditionally forgiving God (1 John 1:9) who desires a loving relationship with you. He is your shepherd, and your safe place (Psalm 46:1). And with Him by your side, you can walk in peace, regardless of anything that comes your way (Isaiah 26:3, Philippians 4:7).

Have you ever felt pursued by God after wandering on the wrong path? What was this experience like for you? How do these verses encourage you?

_____

_____

_____

_____

_____

_____

_____

_____

_____

_____

_____

_____

_____

_____

_____

_____

Reflection continued . . .

_____
_____
_____
_____
_____
_____
_____
_____
_____
_____
_____
_____
_____
_____
_____
_____
_____
_____
_____
_____
_____
_____
_____
_____
_____
_____
_____
_____
_____
_____
_____
_____
_____

Date

LORD, thank you

Then Jesus told his disciples a parable to show them that
they should always pray and not give up.

Things on my heart

Highlights

Prayer requests

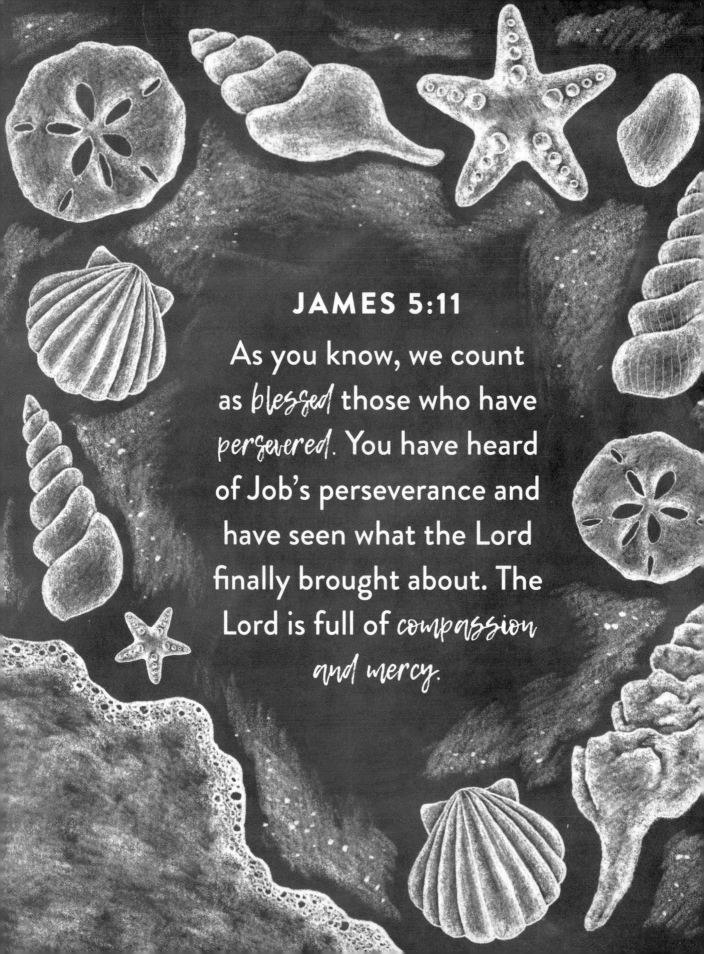

JAMES 5:11

As you know, we count as *blessed* those who have *persevered*. You have heard of Job's perseverance and have seen what the Lord finally brought about. The Lord is full of *compassion and mercy.*

ADVERSITY & TRIALS

The story of Job paints a beautiful picture of what it means to persevere. Job was a blameless and upright man of God who shunned evil (Job 1:8). He endured numerous trials, including the stealing of his livestock, the death of his servants, a fire that killed more of his livestock and servants, the death of his children, and a horrible illness that caused painful sores all over his body! There was nothing Job did to "deserve" any of these trials, but God allowed Satan to cause them and test his faith. Because of the severity and frequency of these trials, even Job's friends questioned his innocence. These events were very difficult for Job to endure, and he felt it would have been better to have never been born (Job 3). But God responds to Job (Job 38), and demonstrates how majestic, sovereign, and incredible He is. In the end, God restores Job, and blesses the latter part of his life *twice as much* as the first (Job 42:10, Job 42:12)!

When you're going through trials or suffering, it doesn't mean God is mad at you. It doesn't mean you've necessarily done something wrong (although this can also cause suffering), or that He is punishing you for some reason. It is normal to have questions, especially when you're going through hard times, but this is where your faith and trust in God steps in. He allows things to happen for a purpose, which you might not understand, but you can trust that He is good (Psalm 107:1), He is sovereign (Isaiah 46:9-11), and He will never leave you (Deuteronomy 31:6)! Scripture says, "For my thoughts are not your thoughts, neither are your ways my ways," declares the Lord. "As the heavens are higher than the earth, so are my ways higher than your ways and my thoughts than your thoughts" (Isaiah 55:8-9). God is infinitely bigger than our finite minds and He knows and sees things we can't. In all things, He works for the good of those who love Him (Romans 8:28), and that includes the good and the difficult. Be patient, be faithful to Him, and trust Him and His sovereignty. With God at your side, you can persevere through life's trials!

Have you ever felt undeserving of a trial you've gone through? What happened, and were you able to see any blessings come out of that experience? How can you persevere through future trials and challenges with confidence knowing that God goes before you and is sovereign?

_____

_____

_____

_____

_____

_____

Reflection continued . . .

_____
_____
_____
_____
_____
_____
_____
_____
_____
_____
_____
_____
_____
_____
_____
_____
_____
_____
_____
_____
_____
_____
_____
_____
_____
_____
_____
_____
_____
_____
_____
_____

Date

LORD,
thank you

_____
_____
_____
_____
_____
_____
_____
_____
_____
_____
_____
_____
_____
_____
_____
_____
_____
_____
_____
_____
_____
_____

PSALM 86:6-7

Hear my prayer, Lord; listen to my cry for mercy.
When I am in distress, I call to you, because you answer me.

Things on my heart

Highlights

Prayer requests

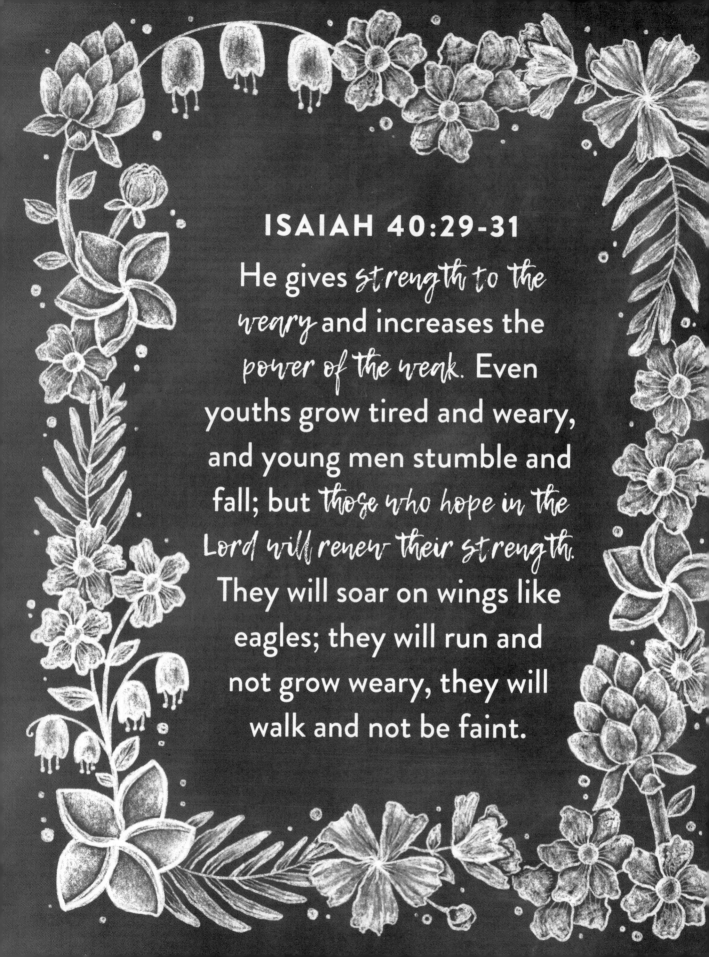

ISAIAH 40:29-31

He gives *strength to the weary* and increases the *power of the weak.* Even youths grow tired and weary, and young men stumble and fall; but *those who hope in the Lord will renew their strength.* They will soar on wings like eagles; they will run and not grow weary, they will walk and not be faint.

STRENGTH THROUGH FAITH

The eagle is a large, powerfully built bird of prey. It has a large wingspan and is often associated with majestic power, strength, and freedom. It is no wonder that God used the eagle to symbolize His sovereignty, strength, and power many times in Scripture (Psalm 103:5, Deuteronomy 32:11, Exodus 19:4). When you look to the Lord as your source of hope and strength, it's your way of giving Him the reins to lead *you*, not the other way around. And big things can happen!

Notice the mention of youths and young people in this verse. Youths and young people tend to be the ones with the most energy (yes, you!), the ones with the "endless motor"—but even youths grow tired and weary, and they stumble and fall. In other words, nobody is immune to breaking down. That is where God comes in. He gives strength to those who are weary and increases the power of the weak—*He* does!

When you're going through difficulties, it can be tempting to take things into your own hands. You might think you see a solution to your problem without seeking God first, only to end up back where you started. In Scripture, Abraham and Sarah tried to have a baby on their own time frame, not waiting on God's promise, and they had to endure the challenges and consequences of that decision before God blessed them with a child of their own in *His* perfect time (Genesis 15-21).

Times of trial and adversity aren't when to figure things out alone. These are the times to lean on God the most by trusting in Him and His timing. He will fight your battles for you (Deuteronomy 3:22, Exodus 14:14), and give you the strength you need (Psalm 18:39) to endure the challenges you face.

Has a decision to take things into your own hands ever backfired? What happened? Conversely, share about a time when your hope in the Lord and *waiting on Him* gave you strength to endure something challenging. Did any blessings result? If so, what were they?

_____

_____

_____

_____

_____

_____

_____

Reflection continued . . .

_____
_____
_____
_____
_____
_____
_____
_____
_____
_____
_____
_____
_____
_____
_____
_____
_____
_____
_____
_____
_____
_____
_____
_____
_____
_____
_____
_____
_____
_____
_____
_____
_____
_____
_____

Date

LORD,
thank you

And will not God bring about justice for his chosen ones, who cry out to him day and night? Will he keep putting them off? I tell you, he will see that they get justice, and quickly. However, when the Son of Man comes, will he find faith on the earth?

Things on my heart

Highlights

Prayer requests

ROMANS 8:1-2

Therefore, there is now *no condemnation* for those who are in Christ Jesus, because through Christ Jesus the law of the Spirit who gives life has *set you free* from the law of sin and death.

GRACE & FORGIVENESS

Have you ever struggled with regret? Maybe you said something to your parents out of anger that you didn't really mean, or maybe you turned your back on a friend in their time of need. It can be hard when you realize you've done something you wish you hadn't done, but whenever you are struggling with guilt, frustration, and/or shame, turn to Jesus.

There is no condemnation for those who are in Christ Jesus. None. As in, *zippo*! The Bible says that when you became saved, you were *sealed* with the Holy Spirit as a *guarantee* of your salvation (Ephesians 1:13, Ephesians 4:30, 2 Corinthians 1:22). Your faith and acceptance of Jesus as an atonement for your sins sets you *free* from the law of sin and death! How amazing is that? Scripture says in Romans 10:9-10, "If you declare with your mouth, "Jesus is Lord," and believe in your heart that God raised him from the dead, you will be saved. For it is with your heart that you believe and are justified, and it is with your mouth that you profess your faith and are saved." By believing these truths, and declaring them with your mouth, you invite Jesus into your life and are reconciled to God (John 3:16-18)!

For all the sins and mistakes you've made, and the mistakes you make in the future, Jesus paid the price for *all* of them when He died on the cross and rose again. He is a faithful, forgiving (1 John 1:9), and loving God who cherishes you! Share your heart and thoughts with Him. He's always there for you.

Do you ever struggle with guilt or shame over your past mistakes? How does this verse encourage you, knowing that you are free from condemnation because of Jesus's death and resurrection? What does this verse mean to you?

_____

_____

_____

_____

_____

_____

_____

_____

_____

_____

Reflection continued . . .

Date

LORD,
thank you

Therefore confess your sins to each other and pray for each other so that you may be healed. The prayer of a righteous person is powerful and effective.

Things on my heart

Highlights

Prayer requests

PSALM 34:18

The Lord is *close* to the brokenhearted and *saves* those who are crushed in spirit.

GOD'S LOVE

A breakup, the divorce of your parents, the death of a loved one —life can be full of heart-breaking moments. Some seasons of life are more challenging than others, but even during the most difficult of times, God is always there. Scripture says He heals the brokenhearted and binds up their wounds (Psalm 147:3). He is your ultimate healer for anything difficult you go through, whether it relates to your relationships or circumstances beyond your control. And He promises to never leave you (Deuteronomy 31:8)!

God understands the pain you feel and shares those feelings with you. In Scripture, Jesus wept (John 11:35) after the death of his friend Lazarus, not because of his death (Jesus knew He was going to raise Lazarus from the dead), but because He witnessed the pain and grief Lazarus's sisters Mary and Martha were experiencing over the loss of their brother. It was after Jesus saw Mary's tears and the tears of those comforting her that He was deeply moved and wept (John 11:32-33). He felt their pain (even though He already knew the miraculous outcome), and He cared.

God loves and cares for you so much that He knows every tear you cry (Psalm 56:8)—and even the ones you hold back. That's how close He is and how much He loves you. He sees every hardship, every heartbreak, every disappointment you go through, and He cares! Give your thoughts to Him, share your heart and your grief with Him, and read His Word like it's a letter from Him to you. When you cast your cares on the Lord, He will sustain you (Psalm 55:22). Let His love surround and embrace you, knowing that He is working all things together for your good (Romans 8:28).

Have you ever suffered a broken heart or painful experience that left you feeling crushed? What happened and did you go to God during that time? How did you encounter God's love and comfort? How does this verse encourage you going forward, knowing that He sees your tears, understands your pain, and heals the brokenhearted?

_____

_____

_____

_____

_____

_____

_____

Reflection continued . . .

Date

LORD
thank you

LUKE 11:9-10

"So I say to you: Ask and it will be given to you; seek and you will find;
knock and the door will be opened to you. For everyone who asks
receives; the one who seeks finds; and to the one who knocks,
the door will be opened."

Things on my heart

Highlights

Prayer requests

Answered Prayers

PRAYER REQUEST	PRAYER DATE	DATE ANSWERED

Answered Prayers

PRAYER REQUEST	PRAYER DATE	DATE ANSWERED

Answered Prayers

PRAYER REQUEST	PRAYER DATE	DATE ANSWERED

Answered Prayers

PRAYER REQUEST	PRAYER DATE	DATE ANSWERED

Answered Prayers

PRAYER REQUEST	PRAYER DATE	DATE ANSWERED

Answered Prayers

PRAYER REQUEST	PRAYER DATE	DATE ANSWERED

Answered Prayers

PRAYER REQUEST	PRAYER DATE	DATE ANSWERED

Answered Prayers

PRAYER REQUEST	PRAYER DATE	DATE ANSWERED

Answered Prayers

PRAYER REQUEST	PRAYER DATE	DATE ANSWERED

Answered Prayers

PRAYER REQUEST	PRAYER DATE	DATE ANSWERED

About the Author

Shannon Roberts is a wife and mother of three with a heart for Jesus. She has been drawing and lettering professionally since 2014 when she first opened her Etsy shop The White Lime. Since then, her work has been sold globally and in stores across the country through the companies she partners with. She loves spending time with her family and staying active with them outdoors. To learn more about Shannon and her work, you can visit her website thewhitelime.com or follow her on Instagram @shannonroberts19.